KU-074-956

ROMAN CLOTHING AND FASHION

A.T. Croom

TEMPUS

REGENT'S
UNIVERSITY LONDON
WITHDRAWN

REGENT'S
UNIVERSITY LONDON

First published 2000
First paperback edition 2002

PUBLISHED IN THE UNITED KINGDOM BY:

Tempus Publishing Ltd
The Mill, Brimscombe Port
Stroud, Gloucestershire GL5 2QG
www.tempus-publishing.com

PUBLISHED IN THE UNITED STATES OF AMERICA BY:

Tempus Publishing Inc.
2 Cumberland Street
Charleston, SC 29401
1-888-313-2665
www.arcadiapublishing.com

Tempus books are available in France and Germany
from the following addresses:

Tempus Publishing Group	Tempus Publishing Group
21 Avenue de la République	Gustav-Adolf-Straße 3
37300 Joué-lès-Tours	99084 Erfurt
FRANCE	GERMANY

Copyright © A.T. Croom 2000, 2002

The right of A.T. Croom to be identified as the Author
of this work has been asserted by her in accordance with the
Copyrights, Designs and Patents Act 1988.

All rights reserved. No part of this book may be reprinted or reproduced or utilised in
any form or by any electronic, mechanical or other means, now known or hereafter
invented, including photocopying and recording, or in any information storage or
retrieval system, without the permission in writing from the Publishers.

British Library Cataloguing in Publication Data.
A catalogue record for this book is available from the British Library.

ISBN 0 7524 2512 9

Typesetting and origination by Tempus Publishing.
PRINTED AND BOUND IN GREAT BRITAIN.

RUL Libraries

74007072

 **REGENT'S**
UNIVERSITY LONDON

Park Campus
Library

Telephone: 020 7487 7449   **Email:** library@regents.ac.uk
renew online: www.regents.ac.uk/libcat

This book is due for return on or before the latest date listed below.

Contents

List of illustrations

Text figures

Colour plates

Acknowledgements

Thanks are due to Karen Dixon and Richard Underwood, without whom this book would never have been attempted. I must also thank the members of *cohors V Gallorum*, and in particular Dominique Leslie and Philip Clark, for their help during research for this book, as well as all re-enactors and work colleagues with whom I have discussed costume over the years, whether they wanted to or not. Katherine Croom has most kindly used her expertise to produce the index, while Roger Oram provided me with some of the illustrations as well as useful advice. Thanks are also due to Christoph Reichmann of the Museum Burg Linn, Jenny Hall of the Museum of London, and Caroline Imlah of Tyne and Wear Museums, for their help with information or illustrations. Last, but not least, I must thank Paul Bidwell and William Griffiths, who both kindly agreed to look over the text, and who provided me with both suggestions and corrections; any faults or mistakes remaining are the responsibility of the author.

1 Introduction

The most common image of Roman costume is of a clean-shaven man wearing a brilliant white toga long enough to sweep the ground. The image is correct – for a small proportion of men, for a short length of time, in a distinct area of the Empire. In fact, Roman costume varied from country to country and also invariably changed over time. It is a huge topic to study and there are still many areas and subjects that need much more in-depth research or clarification. This book does not attempt to answer all the questions, but is intended to provide at least an introduction to this fascinating and complex topic.

This book will look mainly at the clothing worn during the years of the Roman Empire. As Rome was traditionally founded in the eighth century BC there were at least 250 years of rule by the Kings and 500 years of the Republic before the Empire even came into existence. The Empire itself lasted for nearly 500 years in the West and for even longer in the East, where it was gradually transformed into the Byzantine Empire of the medieval world.

The evidence is taken from three main sources: art, literary evidence and the surviving textiles themselves. 'Art' covers a wide range of objects, from portrait statues, tombstones, official reliefs, mosaics and wallpaintings, to the smaller decorative arts such as coins, small pipeclay statuettes, and even graffiti. Although art often seems to provide detailed information on costume, the evidence must still be treated with some caution. Only Romans with money could afford to commission a life-sized statue, bust or figured tombstone, and therefore the clothing depicted is that of the rich or middle classes rather than the lower classes. Just as early photographs in the last century were expensive and showed the sitters carefully posed and wearing their best clothes, so Roman portraiture showed people in their formal clothing and not necessarily in what they would have worn everyday. However, the Romans also liked scenes of everyday life, including scenes of rural activities or domestic scenes featuring the lower classes and slaves, which give us at least some insight into what poorer people wore.

The misleading nature of the artistic record can be seen in the example of the toga. This one item of dress that everyone associates with the Romans was hardly ever worn in the countryside in Italy and, according to literary evidence, was in decline in everyday use in an urban setting from the early second century AD – and yet it is still found depicted in art until the fourth century. The toga developed a symbolic importance that made it the definitive male dress. As such it was used on formal ceremonial occasions, thus appearing frequently in art as these formal ceremonial occasions were precisely those most likely to be commemorated. Art does not therefore

1   *The costume of goddesses. 1 Victory, relief in copper alloy, Caerleon; 2 Statue restored as Hygeia, Museo Capitolino, Rome; 3 Flora, statue in Museo Archeologico Nazionale, Napoli; 4 Diana, statue in Vatican Museum*

necessarily reflect everyday life. Similarly people today recognise a picture of a man in a kilt as a Scotsman, yet anyone travelling in Scotland would be sadly disappointed by the number of men actually wearing them.

Different media will also influence the depiction of costume. Sculptors, for example, were particularly interested in the play of light and shadow on the folds of cloth, and in mainstream art always show plenty of heavy folds, realistic or not, in the cloth. They were not so interested in detail, and so rarely show jewellery or hairpins, while details of patterns or borders may have been left to be painted on the finished statue, most of which were originally brightly painted. On the other hand, representations on mosaics frequently simplified complex elements, such as the folds in cloth and belt fittings. Wall paintings could show both small detail and colour, but are fairly limited in number. Egyptian mummy portraits are more numerous, but the great majority show only the head and shoulder.

Documentary evidence is the second major source of information about Roman clothing, but this too can be misleading. Many of the authors quoted belong to the first century AD, and therefore reflect the clothing and terminology used during one very short period. The Empire lasted for a very long time, and what held for the first century is unlikely to hold for the sixth century. For a start, it is difficult to tell if words still in use changed their meaning over time. For example, in medieval England the word 'coat' simply meant a garment over underclothes worn by men; 600 years later it means a heavy garment with buttons up the front worn by men or women over indoor clothing for outside use.

There is also the problem of defining what the words actually mean. It would be difficult to explain the exact difference between the terms sweater, jumper, pullover and woolly, or the subtle differences between a jersey and a guernsey. The last two of course were originally applied to garments coming from the islands where they were first made, but at some time the terms changed, and just meant sweaters made *in the style of* those made on the islands. Most people would have no idea, and probably little interest, in when exactly this change came about. The word jersey can thus be equated with 'jumper' – and yet in the right context 'jersey' can also be used of the shirts worn by footballers while 'jumper' can not. This naming of garments after the place where they were made also happened in the Roman period, raising similar problems in deciding whether they were made in the named places, or made elsewhere copying that style.

The final source of evidence is the garments themselves, a number of which have survived. Organic material survives in either very wet or very dry conditions, so while very few have been found in Italy itself, many have been found in the dry conditions of Egypt and a smaller number from wet sites in France and Britain and, outside the Empire, in Denmark. These garments can show us exactly what was being worn, but of course they will reflect local fashions and manufacturing methods that may not reflect practice elsewhere in the Empire. Other drawbacks must also be borne in mind, such as the poor dating of many of the Egyptian pieces, or the fact that linen does not usually survive in bog-conditions, leaving a biased picture of the clothing available.

As far as possible, evidence for Roman clothing has not been taken from depictions of deities or heroes. Roman art did not come with captions, and therefore figures had to be easily recognisable by their faces, clothes and attributes, in exactly the same manner as medieval saints. Pompeii, for example, has a large number of wallpaintings taken from the stories of legendary heroes such as Perseus and Hercules. Some of these pictures may be copies of Hellenistic originals and therefore show Hellenistic-style costume, while others that are not direct copies may well use Hellenistic costume to give a historical feel to the picture (similar to the way modern illustrators of fairy tales dress the figures in mock medieval or eighteenth-century dress). The costume of true deities needs to be treated with equal caution. For a start they are simply not human, so there is no requirement for them to wear human costume. It is quite clear that goddesses in particular are shown wearing very specific forms of clothes that reflect Greek prototypes rather than contemporary clothing. The deities were special creatures, outside everyday life, so there was no reason for the Romans to believe they wore contemporary dress, any more than Victorian artists show the Virgin Mary or Jesus in full evening dress, let alone informal daywear. Like us, the Romans usually showed their gods in vaguely 'historical' dress, and little reliance can be put on their relevance to contemporary costume.

The goddess Victory, for example, is usually shown wearing a tube-dress without sleeves, usually with a long overfold, fastened with a single brooch on each shoulder and belted under the bust (**1.1**). An assortment of other goddesses are shown wearing a tube-dress belted on the hips, with a hip length overfold, which is an ancient style of dress seen worn by figures on the Parthenon *c.*400 BC (**1.2**). Others, including Roma, Flora and Venus, wear a tube-dress without sleeves, either belted or belted low on the hips, fastened by a single brooch on each shoulder. On a statue of Flora (**1.3**), one brooch has slipped down the arm, but instead of the cloth forming a natural straight line from brooch to brooch, the cloth is shown forming an unrealistic dogleg so that the breast is fully covered. The tunic slipping off the shoulder is in fact a very common motif found shown on goddesses and mythological characters. It is occasionally found on contemporary female portraits, such as sarcophagus portraits, but it seems likely that it is used to indicate that the woman has joined the realm of the supernatural rather than reflecting genuine fashion.

There was also a tradition for empresses in portrait statues to be shown in the guise of a goddess, while in the late second century in particular there was a fashion for non-Imperial couples to be shown as Venus and Mars. The woman could be half naked or dressed in a tube-dress, while the man was usually naked but armed. In some examples, the man is shown wearing normal dress (such as a toga) while the woman is dressed as Venus – a potentially confusing mixture of contemporary and historical dress that does not mean the woman ever wore that outfit in real life.

There is some evidence, particularly in the fourth century, of goddesses with contemporary jewellery and hairstyles and historical soldiers shown in contemporary dress, but that is no guarantee that the whole of their costume is correct for the period; the artist after all was under no obligation to be authentic. When scenes from the Bible became a popular motif, there is evidence that figures *are* actually shown in contemporary clothing. However, information from the figures should still be used with caution, as the artists are depicting historical scenes and may have introduced what they saw as 'historical' details. Despite this *caveat* against relying on the costume of deities, it will be noted that some examples are taken from gods and heroes, where they provide good examples of costume known from other sources showing humans.

2 Cloths and colour

Spinning

Thread was spun entirely by hand using a spindle (**2**). The raw wool or linen was tied to a stick called a distaff, and then teased out by hand, with a weighted stick (the spindle) used to twist the raw material into thread. The spun thread was also stored temporarily on the spindle for convenience, as can be seen on contemporary depictions of the spindle. Spinning was such a typical activity that the distaff and spindle became a symbol of womanhood, and were often shown on tombstones (despite this, however, there are remarkably few depictions of women actually spinning, rather than simply holding distaff and spindle, and even fewer of them weaving). In spite of the symbolic value of clothes-making, many women passed the work on to slaves if they could, and only supervised the work. Even in the first half of the first century the author Columella complained about women who:

> so abandon themselves to luxury and idleness that they do not deign to undertake even the superintendence of wool-making and there is a distaste for home-made garments and their perverse desire can only be satisfied by clothing purchased for large sums and almost the whole of their husbands' income. (*Farming* 12, preface, 9)

Looms

There were two forms of loom used during the Roman period; the warp-weighted and the two beam loom (for terminology, see p151). The size of loom helped to dictate the form of the clothes made on it; rather than make a long length of cloth and then cut it up into shorter lengths, the Romans preferred to weave the required shape on the loom, which avoided wasting excess cloth. Thus, in Egypt, extremely wide looms were used, where tunics were woven 'sidewards', starting from the wrist end of one sleeve. When this section was finished, extra warps were added to either side and the next section of cloth woven so that the full length of the tunic, front and back, was woven with a slit left for the neckhole. The weaving was then reduced in width again to form the second sleeve. When taken from the loom, it was simply sewn up under the sleeves and down the sides (**3.3**). A tunic woven in this manner would have needed a loom up to 9ft (2.7m) wide.

The warp-weighted loom rested at an angle against a wall. The threads hanging vertically (called the warp) had clay weights tied to one end to keep them taut during weaving. The width of the loom dictated the width of the cloth, but the length could be as long or short as required. When the threads were set up on the loom, they were cut to the required length (plus a little extra), with the excess carefully tied to the weights to keep

2 Woman spinning. Sixth-century mosaic, Tabarka, Tunisia

them out of the way until required. The cloth was woven from the top downwards, until the heddle rod was reached. The finished cloth was wound round the pole at the top, and the weights retied further down the excess threads. This method wasted a small amount of thread, as the warp could not be woven right down to the weights, but these threads could be used to make long fringes if required.

The second form of loom was the two-beam loom (also called a tubular loom), which seems to have been the most popular form in the Roman period. Again, the width of the loom, which was freestanding, limited the width of the cloth. In this case, the warp was looped round two beams, and was worked from the bottom up, allowing the weaver to sit down while working. Depending on the way the warp was set up, this type of loom could either produce a rectangle of cloth like the warp-weighted loom, or a continuous tube of cloth. If woven as a tube, there was no waste of warp thread as with the warp-weighted loom.

Clothes could be made from very simple pieces of cloth, such as two rectangles of cloth sewn together, leaving gaps for neck and armholes (**3.1**). The openings did not have to be hemmed, since they were made from an uncut piece of cloth, and would have selvage edges or starting and finishing borders on all four sides. Another form of tunic, used by women in a number of different ancient cultures, could be made by weaving a tube of cloth on a two beam loom or sewing a large rectangle of cloth from a warp-weighted loom into a tube. The opening at one end could then be part-sewn or held together by brooches to form neck and arm holes (a tube-dress, or Greek *peplos*; **3.5**). Once again, as there was no need to cut the cloth, there was no need for hems. A surviving example of a tube-dress from Iron Age Denmark was made of a tubular piece of cloth 5ft

3 Tunic forms, showing seams (diagonal shading) and openings (black ovals). 1-2 Tunics made from rectangles of cloth; 3-4 Long-sleeved tunics, showing layout of cloth on the loom; 5 Tube-dress as made from rectangle of cloth. Drawn by R. Oram

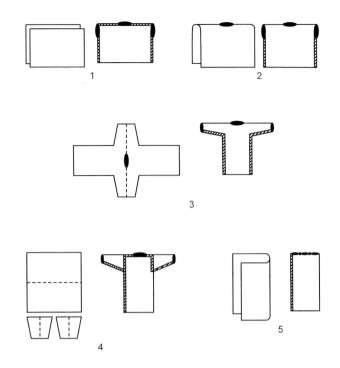

7in (1.7m) long and 9ft (2.7m) in diameter (the great diameter being required as no armholes are cut in this form of tunic, and the cloth has to reach from shoulder, right under the arm, and back to the shoulder again, on both sides). More elaborate forms of clothes – for example, long-sleeved tunics, or the toga, or cloaks with a curved edge – could also be woven to shape on the loom, resulting in proper selvage edges, which are stronger than a sewn hem. However, some surviving tunics do have their edges folded back and sewn which, if it is not simply re-use of cloth, suggests some webs of cloth were cut up for use.

Cloth

The most commonly used fabrics were wool and linen, but other materials were known such as silk for the rich, goat-hair cloth and cotton. Non-woven materials used included felt, leather and fur, as well as knotted fabrics such as sprang-work, knitting and netting. Pliny mentions a number of plants used for producing cloth in different parts of the Empire, such as esparto grass in Spain, as well as a very special form of linen that would not burn (asbestos cloth: *Nat. Hist.* 19.4.19).

The Romans could produce a wide range of different weave patterns in their cloth, and weave cloth to whatever thickness was required. Martial describes thick tunics from Padua made of 'triple twill [that] uses up many a fleece and only a saw can cut them' (*Ep.* 14.143) while other authors refer to cloth so thin it was transparent.

Wool was the most commonly used material, closely followed by linen. Pliny's discussion of linen from different areas suggests that white was the preferred colour, the more brilliant the better (*Nat. Hist.* 19.2). Wool was considered to be softer than linen, and the best linen is compared to wool: 'no flax is more brilliantly white or more closely resembles wool [than Pelignian flax]' (*Nat. Hist.* 19.2.13). Silk was popular because it could be woven into a very fine, lightweight cloth. It was worn by both women and men, although it was always seen as rather decadent. It was hugely expensive since it had to be imported into the Empire from China; during the late third century 'a pound of silk was worth a pound of gold', and was thus literally worth its weight in gold (SHA *Aurelianus* 45.5). Cloth was frequently made of half silk and half linen or wool to cut down the cost.

Luxury garments

There are repeated references to garments woven with gold thread from the time of the Republic onwards. Nero, for example, was laid out in 'white clothes woven with gold' (Suetonius, *Nero* 6.50), while the clothes of the Emperor Commodus sold after his death included:

> clothes of silk woven with gold thread of remarkable workmanship, tunics, capes, cloaks and dalmatic tunics with long sleeves and fringed military cloaks and purple Greek cloaks made for service in the army camp. Also Bardaean hooded shoulder capes and the toga and arms of a gladiator finished in gold and jewels. (SHA *Pertinax*, 8.2-4)

The thieves in the novel *The Golden Ass* steal coins, plate and silk clothes woven with gold thread (4.7). Such silk and gold clothes were the extreme version of luxury clothing, combining two expensive materials, and would have been restricted to the very richest strata of society, including the Imperial family. In AD 169 Marcus Aurelius even raised money to pay for a war by selling 'his wife's silk and gold clothes' (SHA *Marcus Aurelius* 17.4).

Some Emperors also wore jewel-sewn clothes. The Emperor Severus Alexander was praised because 'he removed from the imperial footwear and clothes all the jewels that had been used by Elagabalus, and he wore a plain white robe without any gold . . . . and ordinary clothes and togas' (SHA *Severus Alexander* 4). Elagabalus had worn clothes such as 'a tunic made wholly from cloth of gold, or one made from purple, or a Persian one studded with jewels . . . . He even wore jewels on his shoes, sometimes engraved ones – a practice which aroused the derision of all' (SHA *Elagabalus* 23.3-4). Caligula had worn capes sewn with jewels (Suetonius, *Caligula* 52) and Agrippina, the wife of Claudius, had a military cloak of gold cloth (Pliny, *Nat. Hist.* 33.19.63).

From the first to third centuries such extravagant clothing, even for the Imperial family, was castigated in no uncertain terms. Unpopular Emperors may have been described as wearing such clothes, whether they ever had or not, as an easy way to discredit them. During the fourth century, however, there was a major change in attitude to conspicuous status-display in costume, as well as an increased interest in the use of pattern and decoration adopted from the east, and such rich clothing became acceptable for the Emperor. Claudian describes the dress of the Emperor Honorius on the occasion of being made consul for the fourth time (AD 398):

Jewels of India stud your clothes, rows of emeralds make the threads green; there gleams the amethyst and the glint of Spanish gold makes the dark-blue sapphire look duller with its hidden fire. Nor in the wearing of such a robe was unadorned beauty enough; the work of the needle increases its value, pictures traced in precious metals enliven the work; many a jasper adorns the ornament and pearls twisted in varied patterns . . . . Who could sew precious stones on purple? Who mingled the fire of the Red Sea and of Tyre? Tyre lent her dyes, China her silks and Hydaspes his jewels. (*Honorius,* 585-92, 599-600)

This elaboration in dress is an element of the emerging tendency for the Emperor to stress his 'apartness' from the majority of people by the use of costume, titles, regalia and a hierarchical court. Diadems, once avoided by Emperors because of their association with kings, became commonplace for fourth- and fifth-century Emperors, and eventually developed into true crowns. The costume of both Justinian and Theodora in the San Vitale mosaics show quite clearly how different their dress is from those of their courtiers, from pearl-hung head-dresses to decorated shoes (**colour plates 1-2**).

The rich did, however, have to suffer for their fashion. Some purple dyes had a powerful smell, and could make the cloth feel unpleasant. The Emperor Severus Alexander:

was always eager to get good linen, without any purple in it, for he used to say 'if these garments are made of linen in order to prevent their being rough, what is the use of having purple in it?' And as for inserting gold threads, he thought it was madness, since in addition to being rough they also made the garment stiff (SHA *Severus Alexander* 40.10-1).

Gold also added considerable weight to the cloth. Claudian refers to a consul's toga 'stiff and heavy with gold' and refers to a man 'straining his sapless limbs beneath the weight of the consul's toga, borne down by the wearing of it' (*Stilicho* 340, *Eutropius* 299-304).

Slave clothes

The term 'slave' covers everything from people with a considerable fortune in their own right to manacled slaves treated little better than animals. Households could have one general-purpose slave or an army of several hundred, each of whom had their own strict role. The quality of clothing given to slaves would therefore vary greatly in quality to reflect the status of the person involved. Slaves invested with power, such as farm bailiffs or town-house stewards, and those slaves who dealt directly with the family, would have been given better quality clothes than behind-the-scenes slaves and farm workers. The majority would have worn clothes of a similar quality to those of poor free people and in the Price Edict of Diocletian of AD 301 the lowest quality of clothing is always described as suitable for 'common people or slaves'.

Most slaves would own few clothes. In the second century BC Cato listed the suggested clothing allowance for male farm slaves: 'a tunic three and half feet long, and a thick cloak (*sagum*) every other year. When you issue the tunic or cloak, first take up the old one and have patchwork made of it' (*Farming*, 59). Columella suggests that the clothes for farm slaves should be chosen for their 'usefulness rather than appearance, taking care to keep the [slaves] fortified against wind, cold and rain, all of which are warded off with long-sleeved leather garments, garments of patchwork, or thick shoulder capes' (*Farming* 1.8.9).

Seasonal clothing

For those who could afford it, there could be a distinction between winter and summer clothing. Long sleeved tunics or multiple tunics were worn in winter, while Juvenal mentions 'keeping off the East wind with skins turned inwards' (*Sat.* 14.185-8). A will from Egypt refers to bequests of 'clothes, both winter and summer' (*OP* 16, 1901). A Jewish man had to provide his wife with new clothes in the winter and she could then 'cover herself with the worn-out ones in summer' (*Mishnah Ketuboth* 5:8).

Cleaning and mending

Clothes were cleaned by fullers, who also prepared newly woven cloth by raising and cutting the nap, and washing. They would also re-dye clothes that had faded. Because of the cost of clothes, they would be patched and mended by everyone other than the very rich, and in the later period the decorative roundels and stripes were often removed from one tunic for use on another. Pliny refers to a certain type of wool in Egypt 'which is used for darning clothes worn by use and making them last again for a long period' (*Nat. Hist.* 8.73.191), but when the clothes became too worn or torn, they were cut up and the better pieces used to make patchwork clothes for the poor or slaves. Due to the cost of new clothes, there would have been a flourishing second-hand clothes industry, and clothes were therefore a prime target for thieves. The poet Tibullus talks about walking through Rome after dark, afraid of someone attacking him with a weapon or of being mugged, not for any money he might be carrying, but for the clothes on his back (1.2.26). Baths were a favoured location for thieves, taking clothes unguarded by their owners. Some of the curse tablets from Bath refer to stolen clothing. One Docilianus had lost his hooded cape:

> I curse him who has stolen my hooded cape, whether man or woman, whether slave or free, that . . . . the goddess Sulis inflict death upon [him] . . . . and not allow him sleep or children now and in the future, until he has brought my hooded cape to the temple of her divinity. (*Bath tablet 10*)

Richer clients would therefore take a slave to the baths with them to watch over their clothes. Clothes could also be hired (Juvenal, *Sat.* 6.352).

Storage

All clothes get creased when worn, and linen in particular creases very easily, but it is not clear how the Romans dealt with this. Fullers finishing off new cloth would sprinkle it with water by taking a mouthful of water and spraying it over the cloth and would then rub it smooth. It is possible that clothes were ironed in the same way, perhaps using large flat stones similar to the large glass discs used in the Viking period. It is not known if such smoothing was also done in domestic surroundings on a more regular basis. Clothes

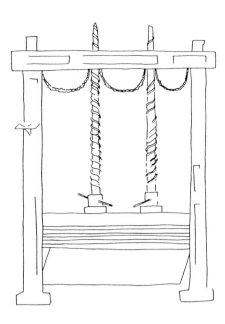

4   Clothes press. First-century wall painting from a fuller's shop in Pompeii

were also compressed in large clothes presses between boards that could be screwed down (**4**). The simple design of most Roman clothes meant that they could at least be folded away easily.

Bags and pouches

Roman clothing did not have pockets in the modern way. Objects were carried in folds of the clothes themselves, in small pouches or in shoulder bags, while the rich had an accompanying slave to carry anything necessary. Aulus Gellius mentions a scroll carried in the overfold (*sinus*) of a toga, and Suetonius a lover's slipper between toga and tunic (5.18.9; *Vitellius* 2). Martial observes one of the dangers of this method of carrying items, when he describes a key dropping out of the folds of a garment at an embarrassing moment (*Ep.* 5.35.7).

Money was held in a pouch (*marsuppium*) that could be held in the hand, or hung from a belt, although this left it in danger of thieves. In Plautus' play *Epidicus* a character has 'a good sharp knife to disembowel the old man's pouch' (2.2.183). A larger pouch *(crumina)* was usually worn round the neck. In *The Comedy of Asses*, the character Leonida takes on a role as a slave: 'I'll act as porter myself; as for you, you walk on ahead as a master should, empty-handed . . . . Why don't you hand the bag over and let it crush my shoulder?' (3.3.657-663). In scenes of processions to bath-houses, the family members go empty-handed, while accompanied by slaves carrying the items they needed, including in one case a slave with a shoulder bag slung across her shoulder (**colour plate 8**).

Colour

Although modern images of Romans are influenced by the hundreds of surviving statues in white marble or by modern paintings of men in white togas, the Romans were in fact lovers of bright colours, and used them whenever they could. However, the ancient authors are frequently scornful of people wearing too bright a colour, which was often seen as 'unRoman'; the Romans had a wonderful nostalgia for a past where men were austere and women modest and no-one had yet been corrupted by luxury. Juvenal comments that 'it is purple clothing, whatever it be, foreign and unknown to us, that leads to crime and wickedness' (*Sat.* 14.185-8), while Martial describes a man who 'loves sad-coloured cloaks and Baetic wool and ash-grey colours, who thinks that scarlet clothes are unmanly, and calls amethyst clothes the dress of women. He praised natural shades, yet although he is always in dark colours, his morals sport a different colour' (*Ep.* 1.96.4-7). Colour was much more important in the past for showing status than it is now. In fact, colour and quality of cloth has always been important until extremely recently, and during the medieval period there were sumptuary laws forbidding people of certain classes to wear particular colours or cloths.

Wool comes in a number of natural shades, often kept as the colour of the finished garment. Pliny mentions white fleece from Italy, black fleece from Spain, golden-red from Asia, tawny from Conossa and a dark-greyish shade from Tarento (*Nat. Hist.* 8.73.191). White wool could, of course, be dyed different colours. Animal thread like wool takes dye colours very well, while plant thread like linen takes it very poorly. Silk and cotton lie somewhere in between. Although the Romans could dye linen, it seems usually to have been left undyed, or was bleached white. In coloured images of clothing, garments shown as white could therefore be either of wool or linen, while coloured clothes are almost certainly woollen. A pound-weight of wool needs a pound of dye-stuff to dye it; for dark shades the wool needs to be dyed several times, and there are often references to cloths that have been 'double-dyed'. It was therefore expensive to produce rich, deep colours, so dyed clothes were very much a symbol of wealth. Poor people wore blacks, browns, greys and creams – in many cases, the natural colour of wool (**colour plate 3**). These colours were also worn by mourners or people awaiting trial as a sign that they did not care about their appearance at such times. Publius Scipio Africanus surprised people because he did not follow the usual traditions while awaiting trial: 'although he was under accusation he neither ceased to shave his beard and to wear brilliant-white clothes nor appeared in the usual dress of those under accusation' (Aulus Gellius 3.4.1). A number of colours held particular significance.

Purple

Purple was one of the most popular colours during the Roman period, and very early came to represent wealth and decadence. Later it became symbolic of the Emperor himself. The most famous purple dye was produced by shell-fish from Tyre, but other purples came from a wide number of sources. Shellfish off the coast of Africa also produced a purple dye, while Pliny mentions that 'Transalpine Gaul [could] produce with vegetable dyes Tyrian purple, oyster purple and all other colours', including whortleberry which was used 'to supply purple dye for slaves' clothes' (*Nat. Hist.* 22.3.3, 16.31.77). Whilst it may seem strange that slaves could wear purple, this simply reflected the wealth of their owners. Diocletian's Edict of AD 301 refers to simple or once-dyed purple, best genuine Milesian purple, second quality Milesian purple, archil [lichen] purple (of four different qualities), light purple and bright Tyrian purple.

These dyes would have produced different shades of purple. Pliny refers to the changing fashions in colour during his own times, from violet (*violaceus*) to Tarentum red (*rubra*) to double-dyed Tyrian purple (*Nat. Hist.* 9.63.137), and he uses two separate words for purple itself; 'robes of shellfish purple (*conchylia*) and purple (*purpura*) are worn away by every hour of use' (9.60.124). Nero banned the use of amethyst (*amethystinus*) and purple (*Tyrii color*) and closed down the dealers (Suetonius, *Nero* 32).

Some forms of tunics and togas had purple stripes, while ancient authors refer to people wearing cloaks, mantles and tunics made entirely of purple. From the third century almost all men's tunics were decorated with purple and white motifs. Diocletian's Edict refers to tunics, tunics with hoods, women's shawls and face cloths, all with purple stripes.

The most expensive purple was that from Tyre. Ovid commented 'what madness to carry whole incomes on one's body' (*Art of Love*, 3.171-2), and it can still be bought today at huge expense: 10,000 shellfish are required for 1gm of the dyestuff. The demand for it was huge, and Pliny laments that from being a famous nation state 'the entire renown of Tyre now consists in a shellfish and a purple dye' (*Nat. Hist.* 5.17.76). Although it produced a rich purple colour, it was equally famous for its terrible smell, so that while wearers might look impressive, people could smell them coming from a long way off. Martial refers to a woman who wore purple clothes day and night so that the smell of the dye concealed her own body odour (*Ep.* 9.62.1-4; see also 2.16.3, 4.4.6).

For much of the time, anyone who could afford purple cloth could buy it, but once in a while, Emperors tried to restrict certain shades of dye and all-purple clothes to their own use. When Nero saw a matron wearing purple at one of his recitals during the period when he had banned anyone other than himself from wearing it, he had her dragged out 'and stripped on the spot, not only of her garment, but also her property' (Suetonius, *Nero* 32). In the late period a concept of 'imperial robes' was developed, whereby certain designs of clothes, probably made of silk dyed with Tyrian purple, could only be worn by the Emperor. Hence, in the mid-fourth century a man was ruined because one of his guests had pointed out how he could use the wide purple edges of the table- and couch-covers to make a purple robe such as was worn only by the Emperor, and the host was thus suspected of having Imperial ambitions (Ammianus Marcellinus 26.8.8). Government dying and weaving workshops were set up in Tyre, and laws were repeatedly passed trying to restrict certain grades of purple clothes to Imperial use only. Possession of 'Imperial' garments was considered to be high treason, and could, and did, result in death.

It is clear, however, that throughout the Empire, it was only ever certain shades of purple, or forms of purple clothes, that were forbidden, and that there was never a blanket ban on *all* purple. Some late Emperors realised that purple clothes alone did not make an Emperor, and the Emperor Julian not only dismissed the case of a man who had had imperial robes made for himself, but even sent him some purple shoes to show that he did not feel threatened by purple clothes (Ammianus Marcellinus 22.9.11). The Byzantine Emperor Leo later declared:

> I do not know for what reason former Emperors, who were all clad in purple, established the rule that nothing of this kind should be sold and did not even allow anyone to either purchase or sell stuffs of this colour. . . . For what evil

could result, even if everyone wore purple, and the distinction of Majesty was thereby, to a certain extent, impaired? . . . . We hereby decree that the sale of small fragments and scraps of purple cloth, which afford means of ostentation to our subjects, shall not be prohibited. (*Constitution* 80)

Scarlet

Although some translations freely use purple and scarlet interchangeably, it is clear that the Romans considered them to be separate colours, even if scarlet was considered to be almost as decadent as purple itself. Martial refers to both scarlet and purple when talking about extravagant clothing (*Ep.* 4.28.1, 5.23.5-6), and it is clear it also had Imperial significance as well, no doubt because of its cost. Fronto, writing to Marcus Aurelius, refers to him and his adoptive father as being 'bound to wear purple and scarlet', while the Emperor Commodus gave the title of Caesar to Albinus and wrote: '[so] that you may receive some definite symbol of an Emperor's majesty, I authorize you to wear both at the present time and at my court the scarlet mantle' (SHA *Clodius Albinus* 2.5). *Coccum*, considered to be a berry by the Romans but now known to have been the insect kermes, was used in the east to produce the scarlet colour for generals' cloaks (Pliny, *Nat. Hist.* 22.3.3). Red is always associated with the Roman army, but research by N. Fuentes suggests that it may only have been worn by officers, including centurions, while the common soldiers wore white.

White

The word for 'candidate' (*candidatus*) came from the word *candidus* meaning the dazzling snow-white toga which a politician would wear to stress his purity. Such white clothing was worn whenever the wearer wanted to impress, as well as at ceremonies and holidays such as weddings and birthday meals (Horace, *Sat.* 2.2.60-2; Claudian, *Epithalamium* 295). Another word, *albus,* was used for a less brilliant white. As well as bleaching, fullers used both rootlet juice (possibly the plant called dyer's rocket) and sulphur to make woollen cloth both brilliant-white and particularly soft (Pliny, *Nat. Hist.* 19.18.48; 35.50.175). Cloth was draped over a frame and the sulphur burnt underneath it, although this method did have a habit of turning the cloth yellow after a while, and could hardly have smelt much better than the shellfish purple.

Black

There were also two terms for black: *ater*, a dull matt black and *niger*, a glossy black. Blacks, greys and dark colours generally were the colour of mourning and misfortune. The fifth-century writer Prudentius describes people trying to show remorse to an angry Christ: 'the matron, taking off her necklaces, puts on dark clothes, and instead of jewels and silk, covers her flowing hair with foul ashes. The fathers wear the dark clothes of mourning, all unbelted; the common crowd put on coarse haircloth in lamentation; the maids, with unkempt hair shaggy like a beast's, cover their face with black veils. The king himself, pulling away the brooch, tore his cloak of Coan purple into pieces, and took off his bright jewels' (*The Daily Round*, 7).

Prices

Clothing in the Roman world – and, indeed, throughout history up until the second half of this century – was expensive in a way difficult to understand now. Producing enough thread to make even a simple tunic using nothing more than a drop spindle was a major undertaking, and the finished garments were correspondingly expensive. Clothing was seen as something of value, and as such is found mentioned in marriage settlements, contracts and wills, some numbers of which have been found in Egypt. The sixth-century will of Falvius Pousi includes clothes:

> I also wish the said mistress Manna to have the third part of all my clothes, both winter and summer, and the other two-thirds of the said clothes I wish to be given to Sambas and Julianus . . . . because of their devotion to me. [To] Cyria . . . . the articles of female clothing found in my house . . . . [To] Manna the third share of my clothes, both winter and summer. (*OP* 16, 1901)

A marriage settlement dated AD 260 describes a dowry made up solely of gold jewellery and clothing, consisting of 'a silvery striped Dalmatian veil worth 260 *drachmae*, a white, single, tasselled striped frock worth 160 *drachmae*, a turquoise-coloured Dalmatian veil worth 100 *drachmae*, another white Dalmatian veil with a purple border worth 100 *drachmae*' (*OP* 10, 1273). A first-century apprenticeship contract with a weaver includes clothing to be given as payment: 'the boy being maintained and clothed by the teacher Seuthes . . . . after the period he is to give the boy on his departure a tunic worth 12 *drachmae*, or the 12 *drachmae* themselves.' (*OP* 41, 2971)

Diocletian's Edict

Of particular interest is the Edict of the Emperor Diocletian published in AD 301. This lists the maximum price that could be charged for a large number of items, from a single needle to a donkey-load of firewood, and including a large number of different clothes. The price given is always the *maximum* price, and it is not clear how strictly or for how long it was followed, but it gives an insight into comparative prices at the time it was written. In the section on clothes a range of prices is given for certain types of clothes, according to where the garment was made, and its quality. Therefore a woman's unmarked (undecorated?) dalmatic tunic 'of the first quality' could cost up to 11,000 *denarii* if it came from Scythopolis but as little as 7,000 if it came from Tarsus. The same 7,000 *denarii* would only buy a third quality tunic from Scythopolis. Mantles range from 7,500 *denarii* for first quality from Scythopolis through second quality, third quality, and three different levels of 'inferior to third quality' to 'coarse linen for common people or slaves', the cheapest of which cost only 500 *denarii*, one fifteenth of the price of the best.

The prices for clothes range from 55,000 *denarii* for a woman's shawl (*mafortia*) decorated with vertical stripes using 1lb of purple dye to 500 *denarii* for a third quality slave's coarse linen tunic or mantle, and 200 *denarii* for a third quality slave's loin cloth. These prices can be compared to the wages of certain craftsmen mentioned in the Edict. A farmworker earned 25 *denarii* and a carpenter 50 *denarii* per day. A barber was paid two *denarii* per person, while a teacher of public speaking earned 250 *denarii* per pupil per month. The prices can be also be compared with other objects in the list. The sum of 3,000 *denarii* would buy a Numidian hooded cape, a woman's third quality dalmatic tunic from Tarsus, a first quality face-cloth from Tarsus – or a four-wheeled carriage (minus the ironwork).

Male and female clothing

There were distinct clothes for men and women, best summed up in Roman law:

> Clothing is either intended for the use of men, women, or children, or is common to both sexes, or is used by slaves. That peculiar to men is such as is designed for the use of the head of the household, for instance togas, male tunics, small mantles, shaggy coverlets, bed coverings, coarse wool cloaks and other things of this description. Garments peculiar to children are such as are used for no other purpose, as for example, the *toga praetexta*, short tunics, Greek-style cloaks, and mantles such as we purchase for our offspring. Women's clothing is that intended for the use of the mother of the family, and which a man cannot readily wear without censure: as for example, *stolae*, mantles, female tunics, caps, belts, turbans which are designed rather to protect the head than for the purpose of ornament, coverings and travelling capes. Those are common to both sexes which both men and women use indiscriminately such as travelling capes and mantles and other garments of this kind which either a man or his wife can wear without rendering themselves liable to unfavourable comment. The garments of slaves are such as are intended to clothe them, for example, coarse wool cloaks, tunics, travelling capes, linen clothes, bed coverings and other articles of this description. (*Digest* 34.2.23)

It is clear from this description that men could sometimes wear women's clothes, but they were generally considered effeminate and derided if they did so. Women could not wear men's clothing. It should also be noticed that coverlets and bedclothes were considered as clothing by the Romans. Cloaks, after all, were often no more than a large rectangle of thick woollen cloth that could easily be used as a blanket. The poet Martial describes a poor man's room as 'a sad hearth unwarmed by fire, and a mat, and a bug, and a bare bed-frame, and a short toga worn day and night' and mentions an old man who used his mantle as a blanket (*Ep.* 11.56.4-7; 4.53.5).

3 Men's clothing

Male costume will be studied garment by garment, starting with the tunic, the toga, outer coverings and leg coverings, including shoes. These, along with hairstyles, will be discussed with their changes over time. Other items, which either changed little or which lack good evidence for major changes, such as religious clothing, will also be considered.

THE TUNIC

The tunic was the most basic item of male clothing, worn by everyone from slaves to Emperors. The length of the tunic could vary but it generally came to the knees and could therefore be worn by itself without any form of leg covering, a point which distinguishes it from any later concept of 'shirt'. In modern western society trousers are the main item of male clothing, so that while it is acceptable in some contexts for a man wishing to cool down to take off his shirt, he would get strange looks if he kept his shirt on and took his trousers off.

In its simplest form, a tunic is a rectangle of cloth folded over and sewn to form a tube, with slits left for head and arms (**3.1**). If the body of the tunic is baggy, it will be too wide for the shoulders and will naturally form short sleeves (**5.1**). Very often, however, the width of the cloth was widened towards the armholes to make the sleeves slightly longer without making the body of the tunic wider. True sleeves could also be woven or sewn onto the tunic.

Construction

Some first-century statues show probable seam lines running down the arm from the neck to the end of the sleeve, suggesting the tunic was made of two rectangles of cloth sewn together, or of a rectangle of cloth folded in half vertically and sewn along the shoulders (**3.1**). A study of surviving tunics from Egypt shows a variety of methods of weaving, which may possibly have chronological significance. One method was weaving from the wrist end of one sleeve to the other, requiring a very wide loom. Another form of tunic weaving required a much narrower loom; the weaving was again 'sidewards', but without the sleeves, and instead of the front and back of the tunic being connected along the short sides they were joined along a long side, so the loom had only to be as wide as the final length of the tunic. The sleeves were woven separately, sewn up and added to the body, which was then sewn up on one side and along the shoulders (**3.4**). Any form of decoration, from simple stripes to complicated motifs, were usually woven in while the cloth was on the loom, and not added later.

5   *Tunics of the first and second centuries. 1 Belted tunic, second-century bas relief re-used on the Arch of Constantine, Rome; 2 Tunic with stripe, wall painting from Pompeii; 3 Unbelted tunic worn by a knife-seller's assistant, bas relief from Rome; 4 Unbelted tunic worn by man in tavern, wall painting from Pompeii*

First and second centuries

Belted tunics

The most popular colour during this period was bleached white, with the only form of decoration consisting of simple vertical stripes down front and back, usually in purple (**5.2**, worn under a toga). Originally these were restricted to certain classes of people: a wide stripe (*laticlavus*) for senators and a thin stripe (*angustusclavus*) for knights. The senators and the knights (also called equestrians) were two social ranks which had a monetary qualification; in the first century a senator had to have at least 1,000,000 *sesterces* and a knight 400,000 *sesterces* to become members of the orders.

The tunic was fastened at the waist or hips with a belt, although usually the details of the belt are obscured by the folds of the tunic. Leather belts with copper alloy buckles had long ends that hung down after passing through the buckle loop rather than being held in loops as in modern belts. These long dangling ends are rarely visible on images of civilians and it may be that such leather belts were restricted to the military. The belt was a particularly important item for soldiers and there were a number of forms that were only worn by them; even when dressed in civilian clothing their characteristic belts made soldiers recognisable. Disgraced soldiers were deprived of their belts. Male civilians, therefore, may have used cord belts without metal fittings, similar to the female version.

During this period the tunics were generally baggy and had elbow length sleeves, although long-sleeved tunics were known: Pliny the Younger commented that: 'in winter [his uncle's] hands were protected by long sleeves, so that even bitter weather should not rob him of a working hour' (*Letters*, 3.5.15). Thick tunics could also be worn in winter as protection against the cold, or else several layers of tunic: the Emperor Augustus 'protected himself with four tunics and a heavy toga, besides an undertunic, a woollen chest protector and wraps for his thighs and shins' (Suetonius, *Augustus* 82). The length of the tunic depended to a certain extent on whether it was belted, and how much it was pouched up over the belt, but the most usual length was approximately down to the knees, although soldiers wore shorter tunics. The upper classes would not have appeared in public wearing their tunics unbelted, unless attending a funeral or a court case or some other occasion when their disturbed emotional state could be suitably reflected in a lack of attention to their dress; Suetonius called the Emperor Nero 'utterly shameless' not only because he appeared in public wearing dining-clothes but because he appeared 'with a handkerchief bound round his neck, unbelted and without shoes' (*Nero*, 6.51). Inside the privacy of their own home, or during such times as the Saturnalia festival when there was a general laxity in conventions, men could wear their tunic unbelted if they so wished.

Unbelted tunics

The lower classes are often shown wearing unbelted tunics during this period. In Pompeii, first-century painted scenes not only show men indoors, such as drinkers and game-players in taverns, wearing unbelted tunics, but also out in the street, buying bread, or looking after stalls in the forum. Stone carvings from Rome and Ostia show a knife-seller's assistant, furnishing salesmen and people at a grocer's shop in unbelted tunics (**5.3**). Wall paintings show that these tunics were often dark in colour, for example, brown or yellow-orange, perhaps reflecting the unbleached natural colours of wool, but even so they could be decorated; a quarrelling game-player in a Pompeian wall painting has two thin, very dark stripes down his tunic (**5.4**).

Third and fourth centuries

In the late second or early third century a new form of tunic was introduced (*dalmaticus*). It had tight-fitting sleeves down to the wrist and in place of simple stripes, it often had more elaborate decoration that developed over time into multi-coloured tapestry-woven bands and roundels (**6.1**). These decorative elements on tunic front, back and upper shoulder were not only circular, but could be square, rectangular or star-shaped; they will all be called roundels hereafter for convenience. As the sleeves were often woven separately, the bodies of the tunics were also often narrower than before (when the width had helped form the sleeves).

Belted tunics

In the first half of the third century decoration was restricted to a number of half lines over the shoulders ending in decorative terminals such as arrowheads. Fragments of tunics from the Syrian city of Dura-Europos destroyed in AD 256 show only these simple forms of decoration, suggesting that in Syria at least, more elaborate decoration did not come into general use until the second half of the century at the earliest. Evidence from the catacombs in Rome show that roundels were used on tunics in the early fourth century, but whether they came into fashion in the late third or very early fourth century is not clear. A tunic fragment with a roundel from Palmyra (**7.1**) is sometimes taken as evidence that roundels were in use in the late third century, but it was found in a tomb built in the very early second century and must represent re-use of the tomb in either the third or fourth century. Such decorations were almost always made of purple wool, even if the body of the tunic was linen, as wool takes dyes better and gives brighter colours. Although embroidery was known in the Roman world, almost all of the decoration, however complex, was woven rather than added by needle afterwards.

An estimated minimum of 20,000 textiles of all types have been recovered from Egypt, many of them being decorative elements cut away by antiquity dealers from 'boring' plain cloth. Very few are securely dated but it is usually considered that the decorations started simple and grew more and more complex over the centuries (**7.2**). This, however, does not take into account the fact that good and mediocre weavers can be working at the same time, or that they could be producing clothes of different quality for different prices. The dating of these tunics must remain uncertain until securely dated pieces can be recovered.

By the first half of the fourth century, when the mosaics in the Sicilian villa at Piazza Armerina were being laid, the decoration on tunics included square or circular roundels on the upper arm and on the lower front and back of the tunic. The hunters in the Piazza Armerina mosaics show a range of decorations; soldiers in white tunics have two or more bands round the wrists, full length stripes with roundels on arm and body, short stripes with or without roundels and tunics with a - shaped band under the neck and a - shaped band following the hem at the bottom and the slits up the side of the tunic. These slits were rarely necessary in more baggy tunics, and during the first and second centuries were

6   *Tunics of the third and fourth centuries. 1 Man carrying belt, wall painting, Silistra, Bulgaria; 2 Man carrying candlestick and wreath, wall painting from the Tomb of Aelia Arisuth, Gargaresh, near Tripoli; 3 Unbelted tunics worn by men receiving largesse from the Emperor, bas relief from the Arch of Constantine, Rome*

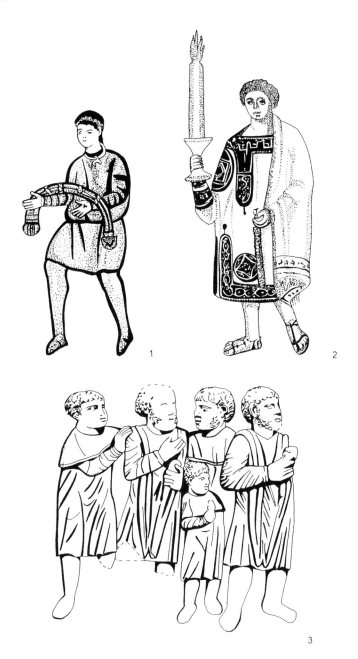

generally only seen on narrow barbarian tunics; from the fourth century they became more popular. A narrow, knee-length tunic had the advantage of using less cloth than a baggy one, but it could easily restrict a man's stride, particularly if he was active as when hunting. Tunics with short slits up either side kept the narrow look but avoided hampering the wearer. Alternatively, the tunic could be hitched up at the belt above each leg, a style seen most frequently in images of hunters.

7 *Tunic decorations in purple and white. 1 Tunic from Palmyra, Syria (restored), possibly third-century; 2 Tunic from Egypt, possibly sixth-century*

Unbelted tunics

The lower classes are still shown wearing unbelted tunics in scenes such as that of Constantine addressing the public on his Arch in Rome (**6.3**). From the late third century, unbelted tunics became more acceptable for other classes: fourth-century catacomb paintings show a number of men wearing unbelted mid-calf length tunics decorated with simple stripes. More elaborately decorated tunics were also worn unbelted (**6.2**). In the Piazza Armerina mosaics, both soldiers and civilians are shown wearing unbelted tunics with decoration very similar to those seen on the belted tunics. The civilian hunters have unusually short unbelted tunics, reaching to above the knee, but this may be a more specialised form specifically for hunters who might need to run easily through undergrowth. Generally the tunics of this period were longer, reaching to below the knee. Those of the civilian hunters and some of the soldiers, both belted and unbelted, have a wide range of colours – red, yellow, orange, blue and green, with decoration in black, red, green, brown, yellow and white (**colour plate 4**).

Some of the hunters seem to be wearing an undertunic, visible only at the neckline. The candle-bearer in the entrance hall also wears an undertunic, worn under an unusual tunic with very wide sleeves. In another mosaic at Piazza Armerina a boy wears a similar wide-sleeved tunic, but it is not clear how common this type was.

Fifth to seventh centuries

The same style of decorated tunic continued through the following centuries. Decoration seems to have moved away from geometrical patterns towards human figures, animals and plants. Some tunic decorations were still just purple and white, but others used a wider range of colours. One example from Egypt possibly of sixth/seventh-century date has a mermaid and a fish in a jewel-inlay roundel in brown, cream, black, yellow, light and dark green and red, while another has four birds in a plant with a square border of hooks in blue, red, pink, green and off-white. A tunic stripe fragment has a double jewel-inlay pattern framing nude dancers, a Cupid and a winged dog in pink, black, green, grey, beige and yellow.

By the fifth century men were also wearing tunics with all-over decoration. Stilicho, for example, has a tunic with shoulder roundels, wrist and hem decoration, and an all-over pattern of circles (**8**).

Tunics under togas

The tunic under the toga always had short sleeves and would be white like its overgarment. Quintilian, when discussing the correct dress for an orator in the late first century AD, describes the manner of wearing the tunic:

8   *Portrait of General Stilicho. Late fourth-century ivory diptych.*
© Monza Cathedral Treasury

> the speaker who does not have the right to wear the broad stripe [of the senators] will wear it belted in such a way that the front edge of the tunic falls a little below his knees, while the rear edge reaches to the middle of the back of the knee. For below is for women, above is for centurions. If the purple stripe is worn, it takes little care to make it hang straight; negligence in this is noted. It is the fashion of those with the broad stripe to let it hang a little lower than the belted [tunic]. (*Instit.* 11.3.138-9)

Although Quintilian describes the tunic under a toga as being knee-length, it is clear from art that it usually reached to the mid-calf. A normal tunic, knee-length when belted, would be calf-length when unbelted, but it is clear from Quintilian and from a comment from Tertullian that the tunic worn under the toga was usually worn belted. It would therefore appear that men needed a special extra long tunic to wear under the toga.

9 *Tunics. 1 Man wearing two tunics, bas relief from the third-century 'Annona' sarcophagus,*
   Museo Nazionale Romano, Rome; 2 Consul's decorated tunic, ivory diptych of Basilius, AD
   480, Museo Nazionale del Bargello, Firenze; 3 Boy in tunic worn off the shoulder, bas relief
   from the Ara Pacis, Rome; 4 Knotted tunic worn by olive harvester, second-century bas relief,
   Museo Arqueológico Provincial, Cordova

This style of tunic continued for a long time despite the variations in the style of toga over it. Then, in the late third or early fourth century, a fashion of wearing two tunics under the toga began. The man on the Annona sarcophagus of the late third century (**9.1**) is wearing two tunics with the hem of one partially visible below the other. By the fourth century the two tunics were even more distinct: the inner was mid-calf or ankle-length and had wrist-length, tight-fitting sleeves, while the outer was slightly shorter, with elbow-length, baggy sleeves (**10.6**).

Two tunics were also worn under the highly decorated togas worn by consuls in the fifth and sixth centuries. The inner, generally ankle-length, often had decoration round the wrist, hem and neckline, but was otherwise plain. The outer, mid-calf in length, always had all-over decoration to complement the toga worn over it, the most commonly recorded being flower motifs in circles, squares or diamonds, presumably woven at the same time as the toga to make a set. A figured marble pavement (dated *c*.AD 330-50) of the consul Junius Bassus shows him wearing an ornate toga in brown, blue, red and orange, with the outer tunic in matching brown and blue, and the tight-fitting inner tunic in white.

The cloth used for the tunic often having the same pattern as that of the toga, it is difficult to say whether the wide band on the right shoulder really belongs to the toga or the tunic (see p47). One example at least shows a different design on the right-shoulder band, with a figure in a two-horse chariot instead of the flowers in squares and circles shown on the toga band (**9.2**). If this is indeed part of the tunic, this tunic must have a V-shaped neck-line, and the folds of cloth seen at the neck are those of the inner tunic (**9.2**). In the sixth century (and very occasionally before) these folds at the neck are replaced by a decorated circular neckline (**12.2**).

Tunics worn off one shoulder

Farmworkers and labourers, including blacksmiths, are often shown in short tunics with the right arm taken out of its sleeve, leaving it and the right breast bare. Sometimes it looks as if the tunic was designed to have only one armhole, but frequently the empty right sleeve is visible in the folds near the waist (**9.3**). In such cases the tunic must have been made in the normal way with two sleeves, but with a very large neckhole, through which the right arm could be passed. To wear a tunic with such a large neckhole with both arms in the sleeves a knot would have had to be tied in the cloth at the nape of the neck to stop it slipping off both shoulders (**9.4**).

It is difficult to know just how common this type of tunic was as it is most frequently seen in depictions of rural idylls or worn by gods such as the blacksmith Vulcanus or Silvanus, the god of wild places, and there are numerous images of farmworkers wearing normal tunics. However, there are a number of scenes of everyday life, including a mosaic of farmwork from France and a relief of a rope-maker, which show men wearing tunics worn off the shoulder. N. Fuentes has listed a number of depictions of first- and second-century soldiers wearing the knotted tunic. The knot itself requires a lot of cloth and it is unlikely that the narrower, less baggy tunics of the third century were worn in this way.

Dining-clothes

Men would change into a different set of clothing for the main afternoon meal, but unlike Edwardian dinner dress, Roman dining-clothes seem to have been intended to be less formal and more comfortable than daywear. They were worn when dining out with friends, or with guests in one's own home, but it is not clear if they were worn when men dined in private with their own family. Martial, however, refers enviously to a man living in the country who only wore his toga on a couple of days every month and whose 'one and only dining robe set has gone through ten summers', suggesting at least that it was not commonly worn in the relaxed surroundings of country estates (*Ep.* 4.66). Two words are used to describe dining-clothes - *cenatoria* (related to the word for dinner and dining) and *synthesis* (used in other circumstances to mean a set of objects). A set probably consisted of a tunic (perhaps worn unbelted) and a mantle, but it is not clear exactly how they differed from normal tunics and mantles, although it is possible that they were generally of the same colour. Worshippers of the goddess Bona Dea ate meals together wearing dining-clothes of white (*Acta fratrum Arvalium*, 27 May 218 and 17 May 241), while Martial describes a clothes press which included dining-clothes as being full of garments in all the colours of flowers (*Ep.* 2.46). They were certainly used by some as an excuse for display by some people:

> During the course of a single meal you get up 11 times, Zoilus, and 11 times you changed your dining-clothes, in case sweat retained in the damp clothes should cling and a draught harm your delicate skin. Why don't *I* sweat when I am dining with you, Zoilus? A single set of dining-clothes makes a man very cool. (*Ep.* 5.79)

Dining-clothes could be worn in the privacy of the house other than at meal-times, but no respectable man would wear them outside. The only time it was acceptable was during the five-day festival of Saturnalia, when the world turned topsy-turvy and all sorts of license was allowed. Slaves were the equal of their masters, gambling was legal, little work was done and gifts given; the toga could be set aside for five full days and informal dining-clothes could be worn outside the house. Martial mentions even knights and senators 'rejoicing in dining-clothes and the wearing of the cap of liberty' during the festivities (*Ep.* 1.1.1-2).

Undertunics

The tunic was originally considered to be the undergarment of the main item of male dress, the mantle, but in time came to be the main garment itself. It is not clear whether, when this change came about, it was considered necessary to have an undergarment for the tunic. In the first century there are a few references to an undertunic (*subucula*) worn under the usual tunic; Horace, for example, complains about being laughed at 'if by chance I have a worn-out undertunic under my brand-new tunic, or if my toga sits badly' (*Letters* 1.1.95-6). In art, however, there are no examples of visible undertunics in this period and if one was commonly worn (and it may be that it was only worn occasionally for extra warmth) it was not a garment that should be seen.

An undertunic visible at the neckline was acceptable in the north-west provinces by the second century. It appears on portraits from Egypt from the third century onwards and seems to have become a feature of more mainstream fashion from the late third or early fourth century, although it was still not universal. Where colour is shown, the undertunic appears to be white, which implies that it was made of linen.

The long-sleeved inner tunic worn under a short outer tunic was not an undertunic in the true sense, as it was clearly meant to be seen and was usually decorated. The two tunics were worn under the toga, and also seem to have been worn under the mantle as well, but generally this appears to have been a fashion for the rich. A number of figures in the sixth-century Ravenna mosaics, admittedly from scenes depicting biblical stories, are shown wearing the two tunics. In these cases the two tunics are always of the same colour, and were clearly made as a set to be worn together. Junius Bassius, however, wears an inner tunic of white, and an actor on a mosaic from Sousse, Tunisia, wears a cream- or buff-coloured inner tunic under a dark red tunic.

THE TOGA

The toga is the most well-known item of Roman clothing, and even during the Roman period it was considered the national costume. It could be worn only by a Roman citizen, but throughout the Empire it was never everyday wear. In the first century, the poets liked to compare the joys of country life with the horrors of city life, and again and again they observe that in the country the toga is rarely worn: Martial points out that in the Italian countryside 'on the odd Ides or Calends you might take out your dusty toga and give it a shake' (*Ep.* 4.66.1-4) while Juvenal remarked that 'there are many parts of Italy, to tell the truth, in which no man puts on a toga until he is dead' (*Sat.* 3.172.177-8). The toga started off as a practical outer garment, was transformed into a symbol of Roman citizenship, and became more and more a ceremonial costume. As with most clothing that has symbolic importance rather than practical use, the people who had to wear it were not too fond of it. In the early third century, the writer Tertullian wrote a book in praise of the Greek mantle, comparing it to the horrors of the toga. The mantle was simple in design and took little re-arranging and:

> there is no necessity for any craftsman to shape its fold right from the beginning the day before . . . . and to commit the whole formation of the *umbo* to the care of the forceps; and then, at dawn, to first shorten with a belt the tunic that would have been better if it had been woven to a more moderate length, and next to examine the turned back *umbo* and re-arrange it, if out of line; of that curved edge out of which the *sinus* grows, to draw back the loosened folds from the shoulder and, excluding the right shoulder, heap it up on the left shoulder, with equal folds devoted to the back: in this way is a man clothed with a burden. In short I will ask your consciences in turn, what is your first thought when wearing a toga? Are you dressed, or laden down? Are you wearing clothes, or carrying a burden? If you should answer negatively, I will

41

follow you home and I will see what you hasten to do immediately you cross the threshold (*Mantle*, 5.1-2)

It is quite clear that in its developed form the toga was an uncomfortable and unpleasant garment to wear, but that it continued in use for important occasions because of its symbolic value as the Roman national costume.

The toga was generally made of white wool, and would have been very expensive to buy because of the huge amount of cloth required. When Martial talks about buying some expensive items, the three things he lists are 'a slave, a brand-new toga or three or four pounds of silver plate' (*Ep.* 2.44.1-4). The toga was worn only by men; the only women who could wear it were prostitutes (see p90). Boys wore a toga with a purple edging round the edge (*toga praetexta*), exchanging this for a pure white one when they came of age (see p120). High priests and officials such as consuls and magistrates also wore the *toga praetexta*, with its broad purple border (**5.2**). Later versions of the toga worn by Emperors or high officials could be heavily decorated and even be pure purple in colour.

Male outer garments come in three forms: mantles (worn draped round the body), cloaks (pinned round the body) or capes (sewn to form a poncho). The toga is a development of the first type, the mantle, and was therefore never fastened by a brooch, the left arm always being used to carry some of the drapery, and so the toga could never give the wearer the freedom of a cloak. Although during the early Republic togas were simple enough to be worn during farmwork such as ploughing – and even during dancing – the later versions were too voluminous and complex for such activities.

Because of the amount of cloth involved it was important to arrange the cloth with great care, and to keep re-arranging it as necessary. Ovid mentions artistically arranged loose folds catching the eye (*Remedies* 680), although anyone who spent too much care and attention on arranging the folds was considered foppish.

Republican

The toga started off as the main garment for men and women, being worn without a tunic underneath, but by the second century BC it was being worn with the tunic and only by men. It was similar to the mantle worn by Greek men, but unlike the rectangular mantle the toga always seems to have had a curved lower edge. The simplest method of arranging the toga was to drape it over the left shoulder with a length of it hanging down the front of the body and over the left arm. The cloth was then taken round the back of the body, under the right arm, and the other end was flung back over the left shoulder. The left arm remained covered in cloth, and was generally held across the body, while the right arm was free and unencumbered. The section round the back of the body could be pulled up to cover the right arm and head, if necessary. This form of simple toga can be seen on statues during the first century BC, where they often show the cloth brought up to cover the right arm (**10.1**).

Late first century BC to early second century AD

During the late first century BC and early first century AD, the toga developed into a much larger garment, using 18ft (*c.*5m) of cloth. It could no longer be put on without

*10 Togas of the first to fourth centuries. 1 Unknown man, statue dated 30-13 BC, Rome;
2 Nonius Balbus, early first-century statue from Herculaneum; 3 Emperor Titus, statue dated
AD 71-81, Vatican Museum; 4 Emperor Hadrian, bas relief dated AD 136-8, Arco di
Portogallo, Rome; 5 Unknown man, statue dated to AD 260s, Villa Doria Pamphili, Rome;
6 Unknown man, fourth-century statue, Palazzo dei Conservatori, Rome*

help, thus emphasising the status of the wearer. The shape of the cloth also changed from that used for the early form of toga, so that to get the roughly semi-circular shape necessary, it now had to be folded in half first. As a result a man now wore at least two layers of wool (four layers over the left side of the body where the toga overlaps) in addition to a woollen tunic. On a hot summer's day the cumbersome toga must have been unpleasant to wear, and it is hardly surprising that the popularity of the garment for anything other than ceremonial use declined from the early years of the Empire.

The draping of this form of toga differed slightly from that of the simpler Republican version. The end section draped over the left side of the body now hung right down so that it touched the ground. Folding the toga cloth almost in half meant that the section that came across the body under the right arm (called the *sinus*) now had two edges, which hung in two loops to the knee; the top of this section was still sometimes slightly rolled to keep the folds in this area tidy (**10.2**). The end of the toga was again brought up and over the left shoulder, with the end hanging down the back of the body. Usually the length of cloth that hung down the left side of the body, originally unseen, was pulled up slightly and a small loop of it allowed to hang over the *sinus* (**10.3**); this section is called the *umbo*, meaning a 'boss', because of its small, circular shape. Because of the huge size of this toga, there was a lot of cloth to be kept up on the left shoulder. Perhaps because of this, some of the lower layer of cloth on this shoulder was pulled out over the top layers to help weight them down and keep them in place (**10.3**).

In the late first century Quintilian describes the correct dress for an orator, and even goes into details about the correct way of wearing the toga:

> There are also details of dress which are altered to some extent by successive changes in fashion. The ancients, for example, did not have the *sinus*, and those who followed them had it very short. Consequently it follows that in view of the fact that their arms were, like those of the Greeks, covered by the garment, they must have employed a different form of gesture in the introductory section of a speech from that which is in use now. . . . . The toga itself, in my opinion, should be round, and cut to fit, otherwise there are a number of ways in which it may be unshapely. Its front edge should by preference reach to the middle of the shins, while the back should be higher. . . . The *sinus* is most becoming if it fall to a point a little above the lower edge of the tunic and should certainly never fall below it. That bit of the toga that passes like a belt from under the right shoulder to the left should be neither too tight nor too loose. The portion of the toga which is the last to be arranged [the *umbo*, although the word is not used here] should sit rather low, since it will sit better thus and be kept in its place. A portion of the tunic should also be drawn back in order that it may not fall over the arm when we are pleading, and the *sinus* should be thrown over the shoulder, while it will not be unbecoming if the edge be turned back. (*Instit.* 11.3.138-40)

As was usual, the state of the clothes was used to make a statement when in court. It was important, Quintilian said, that at the start of the speech, the toga was neat and that if any of it slipped it should be corrected immediately. In the middle of the speech, however, it was acceptable to throw back over the shoulder without great care the end that had slipped down, or to pluck the toga away from overheated throat and chest. By the end of the speech 'practically everything is becoming; we may stream with sweat, show signs of fatigue, and let our dress fall in careless disorder and the toga slip loose from us on every side' (*Instit.* 11.2.144-9). When talking to a judge in private – but never, he stresses, when before the Emperor or a magistrate – he suggests pausing when called upon to speak: 'We must rise with deliberation. We shall then, to make the toga more becoming, and to secure a moment for reflection, devote a brief space to the arrangement of our toga, or even, if necessary, to throwing it on afresh' (*ibid*, 11.3.156). It is clear from a number of comments that he expected the folds to the toga to need constant re-arranging as it had a habit of slipping, which is presumably one of the reasons it was so hated.

Early second century to early third century

During the second century, there were minor changes to the toga, with the overfold being longer and hanging down closer to calf length than the first-century knee length. A new form of draping without the need for the *umbo* came into use from at least AD 118-9, when it is shown on a Trajanic state relief. For this toga the section under the right arm was brought up higher under the armpit and the top section twisted more tightly to form a band sometimes called the *balteus* or 'belt'. The section hanging down the left hand side of the body was again pulled out over the shoulder to lie over the top layers, as earlier, but now even more obviously (**10.4**). It is this feature that develops most throughout the second and third centuries, with the *balteus* becoming increasingly longer, and more visible across the front of the body.

Early third century to late third century

In the third century the *balteus* was developed one step further. Instead of letting the cloth form numerous small, uneven folds, the cloth was now concertina-folded to form a smooth band. The end section draped over the left front of the body was folded to form a wide band – the end of which is usually visible between the legs – which continued round the back and under the right arm. The end section, instead of hanging down in a straight line from the left shoulder was brought over towards the right side of the body and held there while the draping was arranged (**colour plate 5**). When the *sinus* was brought tightly under the right arm it was then tucked under the wide band before being brought over the shoulder again. By tucking the *sinus* section in firmly the broad band could be brought down until it no longer rests on the top of the right shoulder but was actually over the top of the left arm. This same band, of course, continued round the back of the body and was the same section of cloth that was tucked under itself again, so it sat quite firmly and was in no danger of dropping down the arm. In theory, pulling the wide band down onto the upper arm should mean there was no cloth at all on the actual shoulder, but it can clearly be seen in Figure **10.5** that there are indeed some folds of cloth over the shoulder. In practise, tucking the *sinus* section in under the wide band produces a fold in the cloth forming the non-concertinaed section of the front end which remains visible at the neck. The first full figure to the left in Figure **11** shows what the band looks

11 The 'Brothers' sarcophagus, showing the deceased in four different poses.
© Museo Archeologico Nazionale, Napoli

like if the lower section of the toga is only brought three-quarters of the way across the body; the second full figure in **11** shows what it looks like if it is brought all the way across to the right armpit.

Slight variations can have the lower edge of the top fold of the *sinus* also concertinaed into a band, which continued over the shoulder and remained in a wide band as it hung down the back of the body. A number of statues showing this style of draping have twin parallel lines across these wide bands, and it may well be that these represent lines of stitching to keep the concertina folds in place for convenience (**10.5**).

During this period, a new style of holding the drapes of the toga came into fashion. The left arm, already carrying several layers of cloth, and with a restrictive band across the top of the arm, now also carried the lower edge of the *sinus*, forming a pouch across the front of the body (**9.1**). This method of holding the drapery often revealed the end of the front end section. The toga was now often shorter than the tunic worn underneath it, and did not reach the floor as in the earlier styles.

Early fourth century

The style of toga with a wide, flat *balteus* continued into the fourth century, but sometime in the early fourth century there were further changes, with the *sinus* growing so long and baggy that if not held on the right arm, it would sweep the ground (**10.6**). Once more the appearance of the *balteus* changed; it was no longer folded into one wide smooth band, but was arranged in lots of small folds, and was created in a new way. The start of the third-century *balteus* can quite clearly be seen on the front of the body, in front of the right armpit, but in the fourth century, it equally clearly came from *under* the right arm. To create this effect, the end section that hung between the legs went up the left side of the body, over the shoulder, and was brought across the back and under the right arm, where it was brought diagonally across the body in the *balteus*, expanding towards the left to cover

12 *Togas of the fifth and sixth centuries. 1 Consul Boethius, fifth-century ivory diptych, Museo Romano, Brescia; 2 Unknown consul, fifth-century ivory diptych, Monza Cathedral Treasury*

both shoulder and upper arm. It continued round the back and expanded into the *sinus*, to be draped over the left arm. Although this style of toga survives into the fifth century, during the fourth century the formal dress of the Emperor and high officials came to be based on military dress, and more and more often portraits depict them wearing the military cloak instead of the toga.

Trabea

Sometime, possibly in the fourth century AD, a form of decorated toga was developed that became the ceremonial dress for Emperors and, in particular, consuls. The number of men who wore this form of toga was therefore very small. The best examples can be seen on the ivory diptychs carved for consuls during the fifth and sixth centuries. The first design of this toga (the *trabea*) was not very different from that of the standard fourth-century toga, although generally less cloth seems to have been used and it looks more tailored, so that the front end section hanging between the legs is now a simple rectangular band of cloth rather than one part of a large semi-circle of cloth (**12**). In the fifth century this long strip went up the front of the body, over the left shoulder, round the back and under the left arm; it then grew wider as it passed over the left shoulder and upper arm. There was a small semi-circle of cloth that sat rather precariously on the right shoulder, while the rest of the cloth expands into the wide curve of the *sinus,* now rather apron-like, which instead of being tucked under the *balteus* is simply carried round the front of the body and draped over the left arm.

The late fifth/sixth-century design was very similar to the above, but the flap of cloth sitting on the right shoulder had now gone, to be replaced by a wide strip of decorated cloth running diagonally across the body to mirror the band of the *balteus*. It is possible that this is part of the toga, with the band that hung between the legs going over the left shoulder being taken round the back of the neck and brought over the right shoulder, then folded back on itself to be taken under the right arm, in a highly complicated form of draping. It may be that it was in fact a separate band attached to the highly-decorated upper tunic and probably made out of the same, or similar, decorated fabric as the toga. It is sometimes thought that these clothes must have been embroidered, but it is clear from studying surviving Roman textiles that they rarely employed true embroidery: patterns were almost always created during the weaving of the cloth. These togas and tunics were however extremely bright and elaborate clothes, worn only by the very rich: Claudian refers to them as 'jewel studded', 'shining with gold', 'stiff and heavy with gold', and 'twice-dyed in purple' (*Probinus* 206; *Stilicho* 3.198, 2.331-4, 339-40; see also p21). The designs in the cloth are used to define the different bands within the toga; the lower band hanging between the legs, the vertical band running vertically up the body, the *balteus* band across the chest, and the band over the right shoulder are always shown with a border round their edges (**9.2**, **12**), making it a highly-tailored garment of some complexity. The toga had come a long way from the simple mantle thrown round the body six hundred years previously.

Sacrifice

The toga was worn mainly for ceremonial occasions, the most common of which were religious sacrifices. On such occasions it was necessary to cover the head as a sign of respect, so it was important, with whichever style of draping worn, that the section round the back of the body and under the right arm could be pulled up to cover the head (**5.2**). It may be because of this requirement that the first-century style of toga with the *umbo* continued to be shown being worn during sacrifices right up until the fourth century, as it was one of the easiest styles of toga in which to pull up the folds of cloth over the head. Men shown sacrificing wearing the toga with the wide band *balteus* are shown with bare heads, as there were no suitable folds of loose cloth to pull up over the head. The toga with the *umbo* is also seen on a few other occasions in the second and third centuries, including weddings, where again perhaps an old-fashioned style of toga was worn for the special occasion. It is also shown on a few tombstones, so it is clear earlier styles of togas continued to be worn even when the style-leaders had brought in new fashions in draping, but this hardly surprising considering the cost of a new toga. Some sarcophagi show men wearing three different styles at same time. The so-called 'Brother's Sarcophagus' shows the same man in four different poses (**11**); first he is shown at his wedding, dressed in a toga with an *umbo* (second figure from right), then as a senator with a twisted *balteus* (early second to early third century; fifth figure from right), then dressed in the guise of a philosopher wearing simply a mantle (seventh figure from right), and finally as a consul wearing a toga with a smooth band (early to late third century; tenth figure from right). During his lifetime, of course the man could quite easily have worn the two later styles of the toga, and, as suggested above, the toga for his wedding may have been special for the occasion.

13 *Short togas. Bas relief from the Arch of Marcus Aurelius, Rome, dated AD 176-80*

Small togas

Although the length of the fashionable toga changed over time, it is clear that short togas were always worn by those unable to afford the full-width toga. The changing fashion of the toga is based on images of Emperors, high officials or the very rich, who could quite obviously afford togas long enough to sweep the ground if so wished; in the first century Horace talks of a rich ex-slave 'parading from end to end of the Sacred Way in a toga three yards long' to show off his new status and wealth (*Epodes* 4.8). Martial mentions short togas when referring to a poor man, to a countryman who rarely wore a toga, and to the meagre gift received from a patron, as well as the clients of a rich patron (*Ep.* 11.56.6; 4.66.3; 10.15.7; 11.24.11; 10.74.3). There are also a couple of second-century scenes of Emperors, dressed in a full-length toga, talking or giving gifts to the general public, who are shown wearing knee-length togas (**13**).

MANTLE, CLOAK AND CAPE

The Roman concept of 'outer wear' was not the same as the modern idea of 'outdoor wear'. When outside the house, Roman men (other than slaves and the poor) would wear something over their tunic not because they necessarily needed protection against the weather, but because it was the respectable thing to do. Even inside the house some form of outerwear was often worn, while the clothes worn specially for meals noticeably consisted of both tunic and mantle. Historically, the toga and the mantle had been the most important item of male clothing, worn with little on underneath, and the tunic had only been developed as a major item of dress at a later stage. Roman outer wear should therefore not be seen as merely 'outdoor wear' but as an integral part of the costume, of equal importance to the tunic.

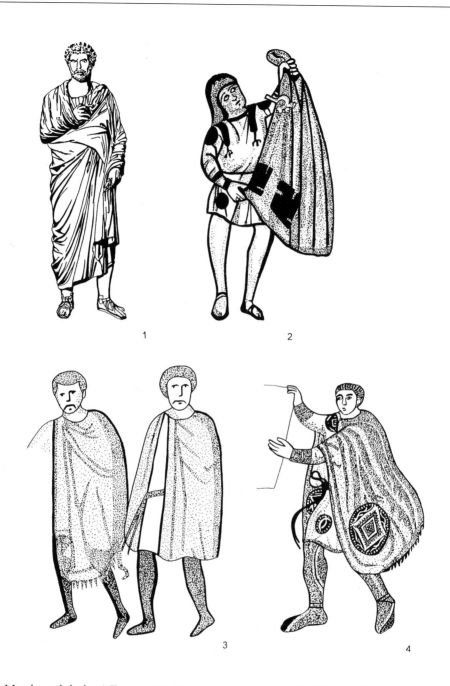

14 Mantles and cloaks. 1 Emperor Hadrian wearing a mantle, AD 117, British Museum; 2 Man carrying cloak with brooch, fourth-century tomb wall painting, Silistra, Bulgaria; 3 Men at the circus wearing cloaks, third- or fourth-century mosaic, Cologne, Germany; 4 Hunter wearing decorated cloak, fourth-century mosaic, Piazza Armerina, Sicily

This outer wear came in three main forms: mantles, cloaks and capes. Mantles – which originally included the toga – were simply draped round the body, without any form of fastening, and therefore needed occasional rearrangement; one arm was permanently occupied in keeping a mantle in place. Cloaks were fastened with a brooch on one shoulder (usually the right) so that the arm was left free of the folds. Capes, of varying lengths, were sewn up the front to form a bell-shaped poncho. Each form was worn for different occasions.

Mantles

The *pallium* was a Greek garment, which came to be considered the Greek equivalent of the Roman toga as a form of national dress. Because of the Greek association, it was considered the correct dress for philosophers and scholars, or those who wished to appear cultured. It was a large rectangle of cloth, draped over the left shoulder, round the back, under the left arm and back over the left arm and shoulder in a similar fashion to the early forms of toga (**14.1**). It was distinct from the toga, however, because it always had straight edges. It was worn without a tunic for those who wished to pose as a Greek philosopher (**11**, central figure), but most Romans wore a tunic underneath that could apparently be unbelted. Tertullian's book in praise of the mantle lists its advantages; it was very quick and easy to put on, there was no worry about the way the folds fell, it was easy to re-arrange, the tunic underneath could be comfortably unbelted, and it could be worn with healthy openwork shoes (*Mantle* 5).

Another form of mantle was the *abolla*, possibly distinguished from the *pallium* by being made of a thicker cloth (although it has been suggested this is just another general term for a wrap), while the *endromis* was a thick mantle worn by athletes after exercising that could also be worn as protection against the weather; Martial refers to a gift of an *endromis* that although inelegant was 'not to be despised [as] in cold December. . . . you will laugh at winds and rains, clad in this gift' (*Ep.* 4.19.40).

Like the toga, the mantle involved the use of the arms to keep it round the body and was therefore not a practical garment for physical work; it is occasionally seen worn round the waist in the manner of a sarong by musicians and men involved in religious ceremonies, as well as by a butcher on a tombstone from Rome, so that both hands were free. The mantle, although an outer garment to be worn over a tunic, was not only outdoor wear but could be worn inside, most frequently as part of the dining-clothes set (see p39).

Decorated white mantles appear in the east by at least the first half of the second century AD, but it is not clear if they were fashionable in Italy at this date. The motifs were generally purple in colour and were L- or H- shapes set near the four corners, while fourth century catacomb paintings from Rome also show swastikas (a symbol of good luck to the Romans) and double ended crosses.

Mantles were frequently, but not always white. Suetonius tells the story of Caligula executing a man because his purple mantle attracted too much attention in an amphitheatre (*Caligula* 35), while wall-paintings from Pompeii show people in the *forum* in brown mantles and men in dining-robe sets with red and green *pallia*.

Cloaks

There are a number of different words for cloaks, and it can be difficult to understand the exact difference between the forms. At its most basic, a cloak was simply a rectangle of cloth fastened by a separate brooch, almost always on the right shoulder, thus leaving both hands free. In the Roman world brooches were functional rather than purely decorative in the manner of modern jewellery, and in mainstream Italian fashion they were worn almost exclusively by men. To avoid misplacing the brooch, they were often left fastened to the cloak even when not being worn (**14.2**). Cloaks could be of any length from thigh-length to ankle-length, they could have a fringe on their shorter edges, and they could have a straight or curved lower edge.

The *sagum* was a thick, coarse cloak that probably originated in north-west Europe and was used particularly by soldiers and country workers and all those who had to work outside in all sorts of weather conditions. The *sagum* was so closely associated with the military that it became the symbol of war, just as the toga was the symbol of peace. Another cloak, originally with military associations, was the *chlamys*, another garment of Greek origin. A higher quality form of military cloak that was presumably distinguishable by its colour and the quality of the cloth was the *paludamentum,* worn by generals and Emperors. Emperors in particular are shown wearing it on marble busts, with a large circular brooch and a thick fringe. Military cloaks other than the *sagum* often had a curved edge, so that the cloth at the front fell in graceful folds. Civilian cloaks seem more often to have had a straight edge, so that the front of the cloak fell in a straight line from brooch to hem (**14.3**).

The *lacerna* and *laena* are two forms of civilian cloak, although the exact differences between them is unclear. The *lacerna* was not as thick as a *sagum*, but was used particularly as protection against rain; the elder Pliny cynically refers to people who raised their price for cloaks as soon as a wet winter was predicted (*Nat. Hist.* 28.60.225), and there are references to them being worn over togas at public spectacles, where they were generally white in colour. The colour of cloaks of course depended on the wealth of the owner, but in the first century Martial refers to *lacernae* made of undyed wool, brown, black, red, scarlet, purple, and white (*Ep.* 14.133, 127; 4.2;14.129, 131; 13.87; 14.137).

From the late third century, if not before, cloaks were frequently decorated in the same way as mantles, with L- and H-motifs, swastikas and even roundels on front and back (**14.2, 14.4**). By the fourth century, the costume of the soldier was that worn, in modified form, by all high officials up to and including the Emperor, and portraits of the powerful begin to show them in a military cloak rather than the toga (**15.1**). Originally, military cloaks were knee- or mid-ankle in length, but during the fourth century they become ankle-length, and the round disc brooch was replaced by a large crossbow brooch (**colour plates 1-2**). The crossbow brooch was no longer simply a functional object, but had become symbolic of rank in itself, and examples have been found made of precious materials, some with inscriptions suggesting they were gifts from the Emperor himself.

Some cloaks were made out of patterned cloth, reflecting the general trend towards pattern in the late Empire, such as that worn by the General Stilicho (**8**). Others were plain but decorated with a *tablion*, a symbol of the Imperial court that took the form of an angled square of a different coloured cloth, sometimes decorated, set halfway down the

15 Cloaks and capes. 1 Decorated cloak, mid-fourth-century relief in silver, Proiecta Casket, British Museum; 2 Ploughman in cape, statuette from Trier, Germany; 3 Shepherd in skin shoulder cape, third-century bas relief, Rome; 4 Men in capes at a shop, late second-century bas relief, Museo Ostiense

front of the cloak, against the straight edge. In the Ravenna mosaic of Justinian, the court officials wear plain white cloaks with purple insets, while the Emperor himself is set apart by having a dark purple cloak with orange dots and a *tablion* of gold cloth with blue birds within red circles (**colour plate 1**).

Capes

In some ways the cape (*paenula*) was similar to a cloak, but instead of being fastened by a brooch it was sewn up the front to give better protection than a cloak, which usually left the right side less well covered than the left because of the way it was fastened. The cape also usually had a hood. If necessary one or both sides could be rolled up onto the shoulder to leave the arms free for work. The cape, when worn in this fashion, forms a V-shape front and back (**15.4, colour plate 3**). Soldiers seem to have favoured a cape that was only fastened for a short distance up the front, either sewn or fastened with toggles. Civilian capes are usually depicted with an opening or seam down the front with the two edges always touching and not gaping or opening up in any way (**15.2**), frequently with spaced pairs of horizontal lines, as if depicting large stitches or lacing. Some are very clearly sewn up, right to the hem, but very often a very short length is left unsewn, producing a characteristic 'W' shape to the lower edge (**6.3, 15.4** figure to left). Soldiers in particular, and some civilians, often either rolled up the cloth round the neck or else wore a large scarf tucked round their neck (**15.4** central figure).

Capes were worn by all classes in very bad weather, or when travelling, and by country workers who were out in all weathers. They were made of thick wool, sometimes with the lanolin still in it to make it waterproof, or of leather. Juvenal refers to 'the rain pouring in streams off the cape' (*Sat.* 5.79), and Martial recommends a cape since 'although you may set out on your journey when the sky is continuously serene, keep a leather cape nearby in case of sudden showers' (*Ep.* 14.130). A letter from Egypt also mentions a cape of goat-hair (*OP* 3871). The neck of the cape is sometimes shown with an extra form of fastening at the neck, such as thongs, flaps or added gusset (**colour plate 7**), and J. P. Wild suggests that the cape called the *byrrus* was another version of the long cape, distinguishable from the other forms by the manner of its fastening at the neck. He also suggests that the cape called the *caracalla* was the version worn in the north-east provinces (adopted by the Emperor M. Aurelius Antoninus, and providing him with the nickname he is more commonly known by, Caracalla).

As Romans very rarely wore hats, a hood was the usual head protection for bad weather, either as part of a long cape or as a shorter type that generally only covered the shoulders (*cucullus* or *bardocullus*, **6.3**). Martial refers to a hood 'contaminating the purple clothes of town with its grease' (*Ep.* 1.53.5) suggesting it was made of unwashed, undyed wool of the type worn by country folk, while scenes of shepherds sometimes show them wearing shoulder capes made of sheepskin or fur (**15.3**). Although frequently shown in rural settings, there are references to them also being worn in town, some people finding them useful for hiding the face to avoid recognition: Juvenal refers to a man stealing out for adultery, his 'brow concealed under a hood of Gallic wool' (*Sat.* 8.145). They could also be worn over a cloak, although it was sensible to make sure they were of matching colours; Martial refers to the dye of a blue-green hood running onto a white cloak (*lacerna, Ep.* 14.140(139)).

Waterproof capes or hoods made of undyed wool would have been cream or dark brown in colour (**colour plate 3**). Other capes would have been dyed; apart from the blue-green hood mentioned above, Martial refers to a scarlet hood (*Ep.* 10.76) and Juvenal to a blue one (*Sat.* 3.170), while one of the gift tags written by Martial describes a thick frieze or felt cape: 'such is my brilliant whiteness, such is the beauty of my wool, you would choose to wear me even in the midst of harvest' (*Ep.* 14.145). The sons in the bath procession mosaic at Piazza Armerina are shown in cream/yellow and green capes (**colour plate 6**).

Although the cape started as bad weather clothing, it seems to have been the most common form of outer wear for the lower classes, while in the north-west provinces it took the role of the cloak. It was eventually adapted by Christians as the dress of their priests (**colour plate 1**, Archbishop Maximianus, to the right of the Emperor), and as such has survived down to the present day.

LEG COVERINGS

Trousers
First and second centuries
In the first and second centuries, town-dwelling Romans would have generally been bare-legged. Full-length trousers were considered the costume of barbarians and would not have been worn, even in cold weather; instead, wrappings of cloth were used on both upper and lower legs. The rural population – including rich men out hunting – had more need of protection for their legs, not only from the weather but from undergrowth and plants and often had their lower legs covered with a one form of puttee or another, including strips of cloth wrapped round in the manner of a bandage. Such strips of cloth could also be worn on the upper leg, either for warmth or protection. Juvenal's description of a woman training as a gladiator comments: 'see how thick the bandages wrapped round her thighs are' (*Sat.* 6.263). Soldiers, including cavalry, wore breeches that extended just below the knee (**5.1, 16**), but it is not clear how often civilian horsemen also wore them, as they are usually depicted wearing only puttees.

Third and fourth centuries
The Emperor Severus Alexander is described as always wearing puttees, and choosing to wear white breeches (*bracae*) instead of the 'scarlet ones, as was the previous custom' (SHA *Severus Alexander*, 40.11). The knee-high lower leg coverings continued to be worn by those in the countryside throughout this period, but the introduction of the long-sleeved decorated tunic was accompanied by a new form of leg covering. They were not trousers in the modern sense, but were closer to medieval hose, being tight-fitting, following the shape of the leg, and with integral feet. A fourth-century wall-painting depicts a slave carrying a pair over his shoulder, showing the belt threaded through loops and the fitted tailoring of the calves (**17.1**).

It is not clear exactly how these leggings were made, but there are a number of possibilities. Knitting was known during the Roman period, but it is not known how

widespread it was. More common was sprang-work, a form of knotted fabric which has equal elasticity to knitting. Both these methods would provide enough elasticity to let the cloth stretch over the leg. Finally, the leggings could have been cut from woollen cloth, as in the medieval period. They would have been slightly baggy round the ankle to let the foot through, and round the knee to allow the leg to bend. Some representations show fold marks as if the leggings are not absolutely figure-hugging, while others, particularly mosaics, show them following the shape of the leg exactly, which might be artistic license. When the leggings are shown as skin-tight, it is not always clear they are being worn unless the image is in colour, such as on mosaics. The soldiers on the early fourth-century Piazza Armerina mosaics, for example, wear leggings of a dark grey colour, and a hunter on a mosaic from Apamea, Syria wears pink leggings. Leggings are very rarely shown with any form of decoration, and usually those depictions which do exist (dated to the fifth or sixth centuries) are of leggings worn by mythological or historical characters and are therefore unreliable, but the late fourth-century Lord Julius mosaic from Carthage does show a servant wearing hose decorated with a line of dots down the front. It seems, however, that decorated leggings were generally not very common.

In the fourth century there are also a number of depictions of huntsmen and sportsmen combining upper and lower leg coverings. They are shown with skin-tight leg coverings visible above the knee, puttees below the knee and a separate coloured section over the knee. The marble pavement depicting Junius Bassus with four horsemen from the circus shows clearly that this section is not just a patch of flesh visible between breeches and puttees: the four wear off-white upper and lower leg coverings and knee pads of dark green or blue (**17.2**).

Fifth to seventh centuries

Hose continued to be worn until the end of the Roman period. A late fourth-century mosaic of the bishop of Milan shows him wearing white leggings while the sixth-century mosaics of Justinian and Theodora show that, at least at court, high officials, churchmen and soldiers were still wearing white leggings, although those of the Emperor himself were purple (**colour plate 1**). A lack of coloured images of the lower classes makes it difficult to say if white leggings were worn generally.

Puttees

In the country rich and poor alike wore a knee-high form of puttee or sock to protect their lower legs. In the first and second century these lower leg coverings are generally shown as being plain with ties at the ankle and below the knee (**16**). It is likely these take the form of a length of cloth wrapped round the leg and fastened with ties. A pair of such puttees was found on a body recovered from a bog in Denmark (**18**, shown both as worn when found and opened out). They were made from woollen cloth with a single stripe and thin woollen cord ties, and may have originally been blue, as traces of woad were found on one of them.

By the third century, puttees are shown most frequently with a bold inverted-V or herringbone pattern in dark brown or black, probably depicting both ends of a long strip of cloth wrapped round the leg at an angle so that they overlap (**colour plate 4**). Alternatively, these puttees could have taken the form of a true sock with a heavy weave or pattern. However they were made, they were fastened with thin ties just under the knee (**17.3**).

Although the inverted-V puttee is the most common type depicted in art, a few other styles are also known, for example, cross-gartering (**17.4**), where a narrow braid or thong is criss-crossed over an inner sock or wrapped cloth. Some sportsmen, including circus riders and gladiators, wear puttees with one end of a strip wrapped round and round the leg in overlapping, horizontal lines (**17.2**).

In the sixth century there are a couple of depictions of puttees worn over the top of other leg coverings and tied with a garter under the knee. A painter in an illustration in the *Vienna Dioscurides* wears white leggings and dark brown puttees tied with a red garter. Red garters are also worn by a soldier in a picture in the *Vienna Genesis* wearing dark blue puttees over light blue leggings.

Underwear
Loincloths

There is evidence both for and against men wearing any form of briefs under their tunics. The reason for doing so seems to have been modesty. Cicero commented that an actor on stage wore a loincloth 'for fear he might make an improper exhibition, if by some accident certain parts of his person should happen to become exposed' (*Offices* 1.35.129). A mosaic from Rome also shows a dead or wounded hunter from a wild beast display wearing a white loincloth under his tunic (**colour plate 9**), while the loincloths sent to a soldier at Vindolanda along with socks and sandals were probably intended as underwear (Vindolanda tablets 38).

On the other hand, there is evidence to show the practice was not universal. Another hunter, on a mosaic from Antioch, is shown with his tunic hitched up round his waist and

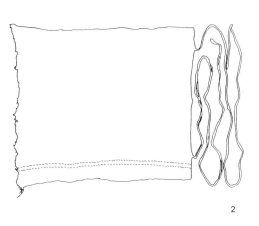

18 Puttee from
Søgaards Mose,
Skive Museum,
Denmark.
1 As found
on body;
2 Unfolded

17 (opposite, top) Leggings. 1 Man carrying hose and shoes, fourth-century tomb wall painting, Silistra, Bulgaria; 2 Horseman wearing puttees, fourth-century marble picture, Basilica of Junius Bassius, Rome; 3 Hunter, mosaic from Henchir Toungar, Tunisia; 4 Farmworker wearing cross gartering, third-century mosaic from Cherchell, Algeria

is clearly not wearing anything underneath. The fifth-century writer Sulpicius Severus relates a story of a Christian reprimanded for indecency because while he was warming himself in front of a stove 'he brought a stool near and sat back with his feet spread apart over the fire with his groin exposed'. Hugely embarrassed by the reprimand, he 'ran almost fainting to [his companions] and acknowledged his shame' (3.14). It seems likely that people wearing short tunics, such as soldiers, wore underwear, while those in less danger of exposing themselves did not bother.

Loincloths were certainly known as outerwear, but these were usually the preserve of rural workers such as farmhands and fishermen. One form of loincloth was probably folded in a very similar way to a nappy, with the addition of two long ends, often fringed, that hung down below the knot at the front, as shown on a simple carving of a quarry-worker found in a Roman quarry in Germany (**19.1**). Another form had roughly semi-circular loops of cloth draped front and back, fastened by a belt at the waist, frequently shown being worn by gladiators. This is likely to have been a length of cloth worn in the fashion of a sarong or kilt, that was hitched up on either side, rather than true briefs (**19.2**). Sometimes farmworkers worked naked when doing messy summer-time jobs, such as treading grapes or threshing grain.

Socks

Socks were widely worn in the Roman world. Some of the knee-high leg coverings may have been socks (see above), but true ankle socks were also known. Martial refers to socks made of goat's hair cloth (*Ep.* 14.140), while a child's sock from Vindolanda was made from woollen cloth (as were the women's socks from Les Martres-de-Veyre: see p95). Other socks surviving from Egypt were made of sprang-work, a form of knotted fabric, or from knitted wool (**20**). Egyptian socks in particular were made with a built-in slot for the thong of the sandal. From the third century, separate socks were not so necessary, as the leggings had integral feet (**17.1**).

Winter wear

Most leg coverings were for use in the countryside, but even in towns wrappings for legs and chest worn under clothes, as well as scarves, were acceptable for those who were sick or felt the cold badly in winter.

FOOTWEAR

In the Roman world footwear said much about the person wearing it: there were shoes for wearing inside the house, and others for outside, some for wearing with togas, and some

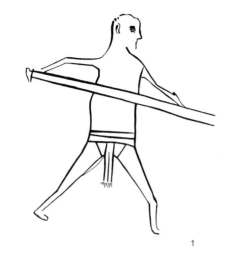

19 Loincloths. 1 Quarryworker, carving from a quarry at Kruft, Germany; 2 Fisher, mosaic from Lepcis Magna, Tripoli Museum

1

2

with mantles, some worn by the military and some by civilians. There were even shoes that could only be worn by certain ranks of men. It was important for a respectable man to wear the correct form of shoe in the correct circumstances; closed boots, for example, with the toga, but openwork shoes with the mantle. There are a number of different words for shoes, boots, slippers and socks, not all of which are easy to identify fully, particularly when they are compared to surviving shoes from the archaeological record or indeed the evidence from art.

Surviving examples show the workmanship Roman cobblers could achieve. There are three main manufacturing techniques; sandals, which are at the most basic simply a sole held onto the foot by thin straps; one-piece shoes where holes round the edges of a piece of leather are threaded through and pulled together, and multi-pieces shoes, where the uppers could be made of several different pieces which were attached to soles also made

20 Knitted sock from Egypt. © National Museum of Ireland

up of a number of different pieces. One-piece shoes were technically very simple to make, but could still be cut in such a way as to form very elegant shoes, while multi-piece footwear could be made as both shoes or boots and included some sophisticated features.

All Roman shoes were flat, without any form of heel. Both sandals and multi-piece shoes were often hobnailed to make them long-lasting, as iron nails do not wear down as quickly as soft leather. Hobnails, however, are not the best things to wear when on any hard surface such as paving, as they cannot grip. Josephus tells the story of a Roman soldier called Julian attacking Jews in the inner courtyard of the temple in Jerusalem, who 'was himself pursued by fate; for as he had shoes all full of thick and sharp nails, as had every one of the other soldiers, so when he ran on the pavement of the temple, he slipped, and fell down upon his back with a very great noise, which was made by his armour. This made those that were running away turn back' and he was surrounded and eventually killed (*Jewish War* 6.1.8).

Shoes worn with the toga

The Romans used the word *calceus* 'shoe' to describe the form of footwear worn with the toga, but we would call it an ankle boot, so the term shoeboot will be used to describe them. Men wearing togas are shown wearing three different forms of shoeboot. The first type was worn by common people, and was a plain shoeboot, with a characteristic ridge shown across the instep (**16**). It is not clear exactly how it was put on and fastened; some of the figures on the Ara Pacis have a flap across the front of the foot, making part of the characteristic ridge, but no fastening ties or toggles are shown. They could be made, like all the forms of shoeboot, of such fine leather that the shape of the toes were visible (**30**).

The second form of shoeboot was another ankle-high boot that was open down the front, often with a tongue; it was fastened by two straps attached to the side of the shoe at the widest point and which were crossed over the top of the foot and wrapped a number of times round the ankle. The straps were tied with a knot at the front, with the long ends left dangling so that they almost touched the ground (Fig **21.1**). The third form of shoeboot had an extra set of straps that were tied half-way up the calf, so there were two knots at the

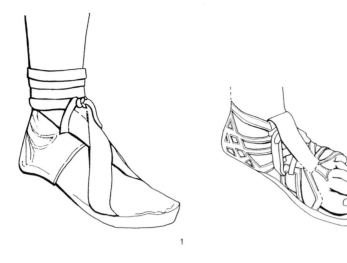

*21 Footwear.
1 Shoeboot,
statue, National
Museum of
Antiquities,
Edinburgh;
2 Openwork
shoe, statue,
Vatican Museum*

front; the ends of the knot were often even longer than those of the lower knot, and were tucked under various of the lower straps to stop them trailing on the ground.

Shoeboots with straps tied round the ankle were for the senatorial and equestrian classes. The exact distinction between the shoeboots for the two ranks is unclear and even the evidence for colour is contradictory. There were three forms of shoe that could only be worn by men of the right social rank, listed by Diocletian's Edict: patrician (150 *denarii*), senatorial (100 *denarii*) and equestrian (70 *denarii*). The patrician's shoe is described as being *mulleus*, the colour of the red mullet, a deep pink. Literary evidence also suggests that the senator's shoeboot had a crescent sewn onto it, but there is no recognised representation of this in art.

The senator's shoeboot, or perhaps only the straps, might have been black; in the first century Horace talks of a new senator wearing a broad stripe on his tunic and '[binding] the black leather [straps] halfway up his leg' (*Sat.* 1.6.27-8) while Juvenal mentions a man 'sewing onto the black soft leather the crescent of the senator' (*Sat.* 7.191-2). Martial, however, when referring to an ex-slave sitting in the senators' seats in the theatre mentions both crescent and shoe-strap, but also describes the man's 'unchafed foot . . . . decked in scarlet soft leather' (*Ep.* 2.29). The lower classes may have had more choice of colour: another man, of unknown rank, wore shoeboots 'whiter than untrodden snow' under the trailing end of his trailing toga (Martial, *Ep.* 7.33.1-2).

The shoeboot was worn with the toga throughout the Roman period, with the characteristic crossed straps and knot with long ends clearly visible on fifth- and sixth-century portraits of consuls (for example, see **9.2, 12**).

Boots

The closed boots (*pero*) was worn throughout the Roman period, and may have been very little different to the first form of shoeboot described above. The men at the baker's shop in the Pompeian wallpainting wear dark brown ankle boots (**colour plate 3**). In the early Empire, they were worn particularly by poor people or country folk, and Juvenal refers to 'the man who is not ashamed to wear high boots in time of frost' (*Sat.* 14.185).

Openwork shoes

Openwork shoes, made by cutting leather into a number of straps, were also worn by men (**21.2**). Openwork shoes in particular were worn with the Greek mantle, and Tertullian praises them for being more healthy than the enclosed shoe worn with the toga (*Mantle* 5.3).

Military openwork footwear

The most extreme form of openwork shoe is the *caliga* worn by soldiers in the first century. From the second century the military wore more enclosed boots or shoes where the straps were integral to the shoes and were laced through loops cut in the uppers, similar to the civilian openwork shoes, but usually more sturdy (**16**). In the fourth century, soldiers and civilians seem to have worn the same design of shoe.

House shoes

There were separate forms of shoes or sandals that were worn inside the house and only rarely outside. When dining at a friend's house, outside shoes were exchanged for thinner house shoes; those rich enough brought a slave to carry their shoes for them, and to look after their outdoor shoes while they ate. Martial refers to a man at the baths hoping for an invitation to dinner already wearing his house shoes (*Ep.* 12.82.6). These house shoes are often described by the word *soleas*, which Aulus Gellius described thus: 'in general all kinds of footwear which cover only the bottom of the soles, leaving the rest almost bare, and are bound on by slender thongs are called *soleae*, or sometimes by the Greek word *crepidulae*' (Aulus Gellius 13.22.2-8). Martial refers to house shoes lined with wool (*Ep.* 14.65).

Fourth century

Diocletian's Edict lists a number of shoes and boots illustrating some of the available range: there are boots for mule drivers or farmworkers, boots for soldiers (both noted as being sold without hobnails, suggesting they had to be bought separately), shoes for soldiers, Gallic sandals, Gallic sandals for farmworkers (double-soled), Gallic sandals for runners and *socci* (of the first quality). Babylonian sandals, Babylonian *socci*, Phoenician *socci*, gilded oxhide shoes and wool-lined oxhide sandals are also mentioned, without being identified by the intended sex of the wearer.

From the fourth century men wore sandals when they were bare-legged, such as when they were inside the house (**22.1, colour plate 8**) and shoes when they wore hose. These shoes were enclosed over the toes and round the heel, and tied at the ankle, and seem to be almost exclusively black in colour (**22.2**). In the mosaic of Justinian's court, the same style of shoe is worn by soldiers, high officials and churchmen, all in black. The Emperor himself wears purple hose and red shoes decorated with pearls and blue stones set in gold.

Socci

It is difficult to distinguish in literature between cloth shoes worn as outer wear, and socks, worn in shoes and boots. Translations usually refer to the *soccus*, worn by comedians in particular, as a cloth shoe, despite the fact that a cloth shoe must have had a very short life and cloth was expensive. Although a number of Roman socks have been found, some scholars are reluctant to believe that Romans commonly wore socks in their shoes or sandals.

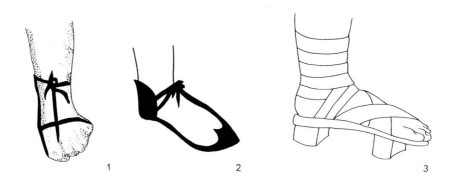

22 Footwear. 1 Sandal worn by slave, mosaic from Piazza Armerina, Sicily; 2 Shoe worn by a bishop, mosaic from Milan, Italy; 3 Clogs worn by watercarrier, Hellenistic statuette, Vienna Kunsthistorisches Museum

Clogs and pattens

Footwear could be made from woven palm and other material, but on the whole was made of vegetable- or alum-tanned leather, and would not have been very waterproof. Wet shoes grow soggy, as many a modern re-enactor knows, and a wet shoe is sometimes used in literature as an example of something loose or baggy (Martial, *Ep.* 11.21.4), while loose shoes invited derision (Ovid, *Art of Love* 1.514-6). People working out in the countryside, during the winter in particular, needed some form of footwear to keep out the wet and mud. Farmworkers wore wooden soled shoes, and Cato suggests slaves should be given a good pair every other year (*Farming*, 59.135.1). This type of clog is shown being worn by a Hellenistic statue of a water-carrier in Vienna's Kunsthistorisches Museum (**22.3**). The shoes have a wooden sole with raised blocks under the heel and the widest part of the foot and are held on by straps of leather tied over the foot and round the ankle. Large numbers of similar wooden soles have been found on waterlogged sites, and some at least were slip-ons, with a wide leather band over the foot sewn or nailed onto the sole. Some were probably used in bathhouses. It is not known if these wooden soled shoes were always worn as clogs, or if they could also be used as pattens (worn over other footwear to protect them from mud or wet).

In the countryside, people probably often also went unshod, although such people are generally rarely shown in art. In portrait statues, however, being barefoot was often a sign that the person was divine, pious or a hero.

HAIRSTLES AND HATS

Hair styles

Male fashions in hair followed that of the Emperor to a certain extent, but not as closely as fashionable women followed the hairstyles of the Imperial ladies. While the majority of

1 *The Emperor Justinian and his court, mosaic of AD 546-8, San Vitale, Ravenna.*
© Scala, Florence

2 *The Empress Theodora and her court, mosaic of AD 546-8, San Vitale, Ravenna.*
© Scala, Florence

3   Men at a bakery, wall painting from Pompeii. © Museo Archeologico Nazionale, Napoli

4 Hunters, mosaic from Piazza Armerina, Sicily. © Sonia Halliday Photographs

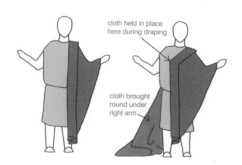

cloth held in place
here during draping

cloth brought
round under
right arm

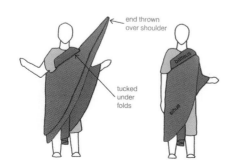

end thrown
over shoulder

tucked
under
folds

5 The method of putting on a third-century toga. For reference, the end of the toga that hangs down the front of the body has been coloured blue, and the end that hangs down the back of the body has been coloured red. Drawn by R. Oram

6 *A reconstruction of a cape.*
   © cohors V Gallorum

7 *This reconstruction of the cape has an
   extra piece of cloth at the neck that can be
   unfastened, producing a higher neckline to
   give better protection in bad weather.*
   © cohors V Gallorum

8 *Family and slaves in procession to baths, mosaic from Piazza Armerina, Sicily.*
   © Sonia Halliday photographs

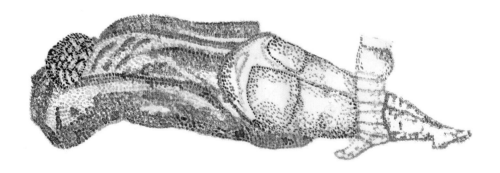

9 *A dead or wounded hunter, mosaic, Museo Borghese, Rome*

10 Coin portraits. From left: top line – Trajan AD 101–2; Hadrian AD 134–8; Septimius Severus AD 205. Bottom line – Severus Alexander AD 231–5; Constantius I c.AD 300; Constantine I c.AD 321. © Arbeia Roman Fort, South Shields

11 Reconstruction of a stola *in wool, worn over a gap-sleeved tunic in linen.*
© cohors V Gallorum

12 Reconstruction of a gap-sleeved tunic in silk.
© cohors V Gallorum

13 Woman having her hair dressed, watched over by mythological figures.
© Museo Archeologico Nazionale, Napoli

14 Portrait of a woman from Hawara, Egypt, c.AD 100–20. British Museum EA74712.
© Copyright The British Museum

15 *Painted shroud of a woman, Egypt. The Metropolitan Museum of Art, Rogers Fund, 1909 (09.181.8).* Photograph © 1996 The Metropolitan Museum of Art

16 *(top right) Gold and glass portrait roundel of unknown family. Third- or fourth-century, Museo Civico dell'età Cristiana, Brescia.* © Scala, Florence

17 *(bottom right) Reconstructed leather briefs of the patterns of examples found at Queen's Street and Shadwell, London* © cohors V Gallorum

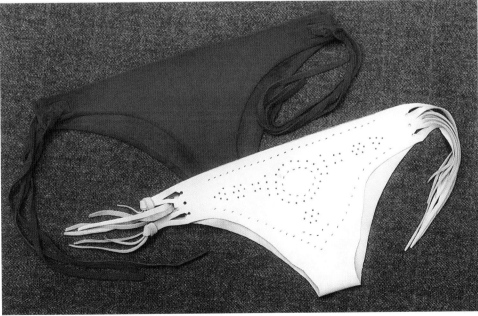

18 Women exercising before a bath, wearing briefs and breastbands, mosaic from Piazza Armerina, Sicily ©Sonia Halliday Photographs

19 Coin portraits. From left: top line – Faustina I AD 141+; Faustina II AD 145-6. Bottom line – Lucilla AD 161-80; Julia Mamaea AD 222-35. © Arbeia Roman Fort, South Shields

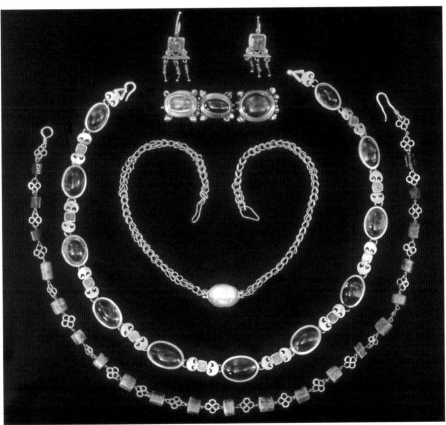

20 Jewellery of first- to third-century date, including three necklaces, a pair of ear-rings and a fragment of bracelet. They are made from gold, pearls, emeralds, citrines, amethysts, garnets and quartz. © Copyright The British Museum

21 *Fragment of child's decorated tunic from Egypt, showing one sleeve and a tuck at waist height.*
© Laing Art Gallery, Newcastle Upon Tyne

22 *Tombstone portrait of Regina, shown wearing a Gallic coat, Arbeia Roman Fort and Museum.* © Arbeia Roman Fort, South Shields

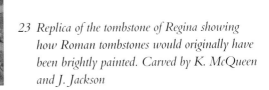

23 *Replica of the tombstone of Regina showing how Roman tombstones would originally have been brightly painted. Carved by K. McQueen and J. Jackson*

24 *A selection of men's provincial costumes*

25 *A selection of women's provincial costumes*

23 Hairstyles of the first to third centuries. 1 30 BC – AD 117, Augustus; 2 30 BC – AD 117, Nero; 3 AD 117 – 170; 4 AD 170 – 211; 5–6 third-century youths

female styles would have required false hairpieces if not complete wigs, it was less acceptable for men to wear wigs and their hairstyles were therefore more dependent on nature. Depictions of individual Emperors can often be recognised by the arrangement of their hair and how it was cut, but it is not clear how closely other men followed the style, particularly when it came to such matters as the degree of curl, which for many men would not have come naturally. Receding hairlines or bald patches were also unlikely to be imitated intentionally!

Suetonius says that the Emperor Otho wore a wig, and his portraits on coins do indeed show someone with a full head of hair (*Otho*, 12). Only a small number of people in the Empire would actually have seen the Emperor in the flesh, so the majority of people were dependent on portraits – coins, official statues and commemorative works of art – to see what he looked like, and of course the Emperor had control over these images. Perhaps the best example of this is Augustus, whose official portraits continued to show the face of a young man up until his death at the age of 76. However, men could still copy what they thought was the Emperor's hairstyle, and there were a number of broad trends throughout the Empire.

30 BC – AD 117

Augustus was clean-shaven with short hair in comma-shaped curls, brushed forward into a fringe at the front (**23.1**). The hair at the back of the neck could be either short or long enough to brush forward round the neck under the ears. This basic, simple style was copied by the Emperors immediately following Augustus with only minor alterations. Nero is sometimes shown with a short beard round the edge of his face under his chin (**23.2**). Two of the short-lived Emperors of the civil war period had short hair with no curls, and when the new Flavian dynasty came into power, the Augustan style continued, with short hair with many curls (**colour plate 10**).

AD 117 – AD 170

Hadrian was the first Emperor to have a full beard. From his reign onwards, almost every Emperor (other than boy-Emperors) had a beard until the fourth century, and it is clear that many non-Imperial men copied the style. Hadrian was extremely fond of Greek culture, and as Greek poets, philosophers and statesmen of the past were shown with beards, he may have deliberately chosen to sport a beard. His beard was short, following his jaw, and his hair remained short with comma-shaped curls (**23.3, colour plate 10**).

AD 170 – AD 211

Marcus Aurelius had a more bulky hairstyle with more loop-shaped curls and a longer, pointed beard (**23.4**). Septimius Severus had an even longer beard, sometimes depicted as if it had small ringlets within it (**colour plate 10**).

Third century

The fashion for beards continued throughout the third century. Generally, but not exclusively, men's hair was very short during this period, often being little more than a crew-cut, with beards equally short. The third century was a time of numerous Emperors, many with short reigns. There was also a growing tendency to have co-rulers instead of a single Emperor, with the more important Emperor referred to as the Augustus and the more minor Emperor - often the son and heir - as the Caesar. Boy-Emperors and sons appointed as Caesars meant a number of boys or young men were depicted on coins or official portraits statues. Young Emperors such as Caracalla (29 when he died), Severus Alexander (27) and Gordian III (about 19) are often shown with long sideburns and moustache, or a narrow beard that follows the jawline with a separate moustache (**23.5-6**). Severus Alexander, for example, was 14 when he became Emperor and for the first few years his coins show him as a beardless youth. When he was about 18 he is shown with short sideburns, and when 19 with a moustache and a beard that follows his jawline. A few coins dated to the last four years of his reign show him with a full beard (**colour plate 10**). In the first century some statues of Nero (17 when first Emperor) also show long sideburns and a narrow beard, and it may be that these were always accepted as a young man's hairstyle. The moustache itself was not considered a very Roman hairstyle and was generally the preserve of Celts or northern barbarians when shown in art, but in the third century at least a moustache seems to have been acceptable when worn by young men before they progressed to a full beard (**24.7**).

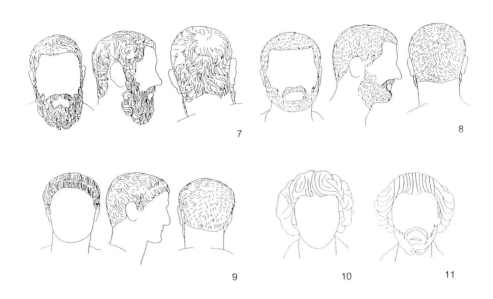

24 Hairstyles of the third to sixth centuries. 7-8 third century; 9 fourth century; 10-11 fifth century

Late third to early fourth century

In the late third century the hair is usually shown as a crew-cut, with an equally short beard that often grows some way down the neck (**24.8**). In AD 293 a new system of government known as the Tetrarchy (four man rule) was introduced, in which the Empire was divided up so that each of the four co-Emperors had separate areas of authority. To stress the relationship between the four men there was a tendency to suppress any depiction of individuality in favour of a communal image for the four. In AD 305 Constantine was appointed a Tetrarch and at this stage in his life was usually shown with a beard like his fellow rulers. By AD 312, however, there were only two Emperors instead of four and in AD 324 Constantine got rid of his fellow Augustus and became the first sole Emperor for forty years. There was a major change in the representation of the official image of the Emperor after AD 312, and from this time on Constantine was always shown clean-shaven (**colour plate 10**).

This change in hairstyle was a calculated move; the clean-shaven face and short curls brushed forward recalled the hairstyle of Augustus and his successors of 300 years earlier and Constantine wanted to be associated with the Augustan ideal and the glories of times past, not with his predecessors, the Tetrarchs. The fourth-century version of this hairstyle did not have short, tousled curls all over the head, but instead the hair was straight and brushed forward from the back of the head (**24.9**).

Fourth to seventh centuries

This hairstyle remained in fashion until the seventh century at least, although after the fourth century the hair was often slightly longer, with a noticeable bulk over the ears

(**24.10-11**). The most noticeable exception to the clean-shaven look was the Emperor Julian, who reigned AD 360-3. Emperors had been Christian since Constantine, but Julian was a determined pagan, who wished to see a return to the old ways. Although having a beard may simply have been a personal choice – he had worn one when young and resumed it as soon as he became sole Emperor – it did help him distinguish his image from that of his Christian predecessors and reflected the accepted image of the Greek philosophers he admired. Julian wrote a book called the *Beardhaters*, in which he recalled the ridicule he suffered for having a beard during a time when it was unfashionable. After his short reign, the clean-shaven look returned, although it is noticeable that during the fourth and fifth centuries, it was generally the usurpers to the throne who wore a beard, in contrast to the generally clean-shaven image of the official rulers (such as Procopius, AD 365-6 and Eugenius AD 392-4, who probably modelled their image on that of Julian, and Johannes, AD 423-5 and Avitus AD 455-6). It is likely that many people followed Julian's fashions as he was a legitimate ruler, but it is possible that followers of the later usurpers deliberately wore beards to show where their loyalties lay. The mosaic of Justinian's court of *c.*AD 546-8 shows the Emperor, his bodyguard and some of his high officials with a variety of short hairstyles and generally clean-shaven faces, while the Archbishop Maximianus is shown with a beard, which seems to have become more and more common with priests.

Hair oil

It is clear from the literary evidence that some men resorted to curling tongs to produce the perfect style. It is also known that they used oil on their hair. In the time of the Republic, Cicero referred to men 'with their carefully combed hair, dripping with oil' (*Catiline* 2.22), while in the first century Ovid warned women against being swayed by men with hair covered in nard (an aromatic ointment made from the spikenard plant), and Pliny complains about soldiers who justified the use of hair-oil because the military standards were anointed with perfumes on special days (*Nat. Hist.* 13.4.23). Both spikenard and myrrh, a resin used in incense, are mentioned as scents used in hair oil (Ovid *Meta:* 5.52-3) and Martial complained about a man 'whose oily hair can be smelt all over the theatre' (*Ep.* 2.30). It is not clear if the fashion continued into the fourth century, or whether it came back into fashion then: Prudentius refers to men using spikenard on their hair (*Mansoul* 359-60) while hair surviving in a fourth-century male grave at Poundsbury, Dorset, still had oil or fat on it. The oil could also be used as perfume; Pliny mentions a man in hiding being discovered because of his powerful perfume, and says that the Emperor Nero wore scent on the soles of his feet (*Nat. Hist.* 13.4.22, 25).

Hats

In the Roman period hats were generally functional, and were not worn simply as an item of fashion until the late third century, although in the first century Statius does mention a hat made of the cuttings from cloaks sewn together as a suitable cheap gift (4.9.24). Protective head coverings were used in particular by travellers and labourers. The hoods of capes were used as protection against rain and bad weather (**15.2**), while wide-brimmed

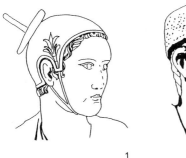

*25 Headwear. 1 Priest, bas relief from Ara Pacis,
Rome; 2 Soldier wearing pill box hat, bas relief
from sarcophagus, Arles, Rome; 3 Scenes of slaves
being freed, bas relief from Mariemonet, Belgium*

straw hats were worn as protection against the sun, particularly by fishermen and sailors
(**19.2**). Augustus hated the sun and often wore such a hat even in Rome, and similar hats
could be seen in the theatres when the wind was too high for the awnings to be used
(Martial, *Ep.* 14.29). A fold of toga or cloak could also be used to protect the head, but was
used particularly when a man was sacrificing and covered his head out of respect (**5.2**).
Brimless, tight-fitting caps of fur or leather were worn by sportsmen and athletes such as
wrestlers and charioteers (Martial, *Ep.* 14.50, Aulus Gellius 2.26.2), while caps made to a
similar pattern, but much more elaborate, were worn by some priests (**25.1**).

From the late third century, soldiers took to wearing a small pill-box hat (**25.2**),
probably made of sheepskin or fur, or possibly from leather (Diocletian's Edict lists a hat
made from sheepskin costing 200 *denarii*). In the fourth century Vegetius refers to soldiers
wearing Pannonian hats (*Military science* 20), while Ammianus Marcellinus mentions a
soldier wearing a hat under his helmet, probably to act as padding (29.8.8), and it may be
that both refer to the pill-box hat. It was also worn by soldiers when not wearing armour
or carrying weapons, and the pill-box hat possibly came to identify a soldier as much as
his distinctive belt, and was therefore never worn by the non-military.

Freedman's cap

The most important hat with symbolic value was the freedman's cap (*pilleus*), a brimless
conical hat. It was worn by freed slaves, at least in the first and second centuries, to show
their new status, symbolising liberty and freedom. Figure **25.3** shows the ceremonial
method of freeing slaves in the presence of a magistrate, with the two men wearing the
conical hat. It was otherwise a form of headgear worn only on festive or ceremonial
occasions, such as funeral processions and during the Saturnalia celebrations (Persius
3.105, Martial *Ep.* 9.6). After Nero's death, 'such was the public rejoicing that the people

put on liberty-caps and ran about all over the city' (Suetonius, *Nero* 67). It is unlikely that the cap was worn much at any other time, as it would have drawn attention to the man's servile background.

SPECIAL COSTUMES

Wedding
While women could wear a special outfit for their wedding (see p109), men had no corresponding traditional costume and are usually shown in a toga.

Religious
Most Roman religious activities were based on the sacrifice of either incense and wine or of animals, and anyone, male or female, could perform the ceremony. Those who could afford to own a toga usually wore it for the sacrifice ceremony, pulling a fold up over the head to show respect for the gods (**5.2**). Such sacrifices did not require a priest as such, but when the sacrifice involved an animal, men were needed to kill the beasts. They wore a cloth round their waist, sarong fashion, fringed and reaching below the knees. It was held up with a belt or band of cloth wrapped several times round the waist, which also held the special triangular-bladed knife used to deal with the animal (**26.1**). Some of the major cults, however, had official priests (sometimes political appointments) as did some of the more private, less official cults. Priests would have had their own costumes, while some had quite elaborate regalia, including decorated wristclasps, body harnesses and crowns.

26 Religious costumes.
1 Slaughterman for sacrifices, bas relief from Arch of Severus, Lepcis Magna;
2 Priest of Isis, wall painting from Herculaneum

Isis

People connected to the worship of the Egyptian goddess Isis, whether priests or followers, wore linen. This was so well known that almost all references to them call them 'linen-clad'. Apuleius describes the priests in a passage where he goes into detail about the worship of the cult in his book *The Golden Ass*: 'the men's heads were completely shaven . . . . the leading priests also clothed in brilliant-white linen drawn tight across their breast and hanging down to their feet' (11.10). A wall painting from Herculaneum shows priests wearing this outfit (**26.2**).

Priests of Jupiter

Aulus Gellius describes the dress of one of these priests: 'he has not a knot in his head-dress, belt or any part of his dress . . . . he must not be in the open air without his cap . . . . he does not take off his inner tunic except under cover . . . . [and the Chief Priest] alone has a white hat' (10.15). The cap worn by the priests was the *apex*, a tight fitting cap tied under the chin, with a short rod sticking up from the top (**25.1**).

Mourning

There were a number of occasions when people were not supposed to take care of their appearance, the most important of course being during mourning. Men went unshaven, or with untrimmed beards and wore old, dark, or even torn clothing. Ovid refers to 'black clothes' as the 'clothing of woe' (*Ibis* 1001-4), but it is clear any dull or dark coloured clothing could be used; the clothes are described by words that can be translated as dirty, mean, soiled, dark grey, or undyed (*sordidatus, pullatus*). Similar clothes were worn on other unhappy occasions, such as when Cicero went into mourning in sympathy with a publicly disgraced relative (*Letters* 5.1.2), the most common reason being court cases. In the fifth century Sidonius illustrates the importance of dressing correctly for court when describing the trial of his friend Arvandus:

> Our man makes his way to the senate-house, having shortly before been shaven and rubbed down, while his accusers, in half mourning and unkempt, await the summons . . . . having robbed the accused of his due sympathy by their own intentional squalor, and availing themselves of the indignation which the sight of men in squalid clothes arouses . . . . Because he had marched into the presence of his judges adorned and elegant whilst his accusers were dressed in black, the pitiable circumstances in which he appeared only a little later evoked no pity as he was dragged off to prison. For who would distress himself greatly about the position of one whom he saw being carried off to the quarries or the slave-prison so carefully dressed and perfumed? (*Letters* 1.7.9-11)

Such mistakes were not unimportant either, as the over-confident Arvandus was in need of any mercy he could inspire since he had been found guilty of treason and sentenced to death, a sentence that was only later changed to exile.

JEWELLERY

Men tended not to wear much jewellery, as those that did were considered effeminate. Torcs, bracelets and earrings were worn by men in some provinces of the Empire, and the fashions occasionally spread to Rome, but they were generally looked down upon as not being 'Roman' and did not last long.

Necklaces

Bullae

In the first century AD, young boys from rich families wore a hollow circular pendant amulet *(bulla)* round their neck (**27**). This was originally an Etruscan habit, and for the rich it was made of gold. There is some evidence that poorer boys wore a leather version (Juvenal 5.165). This tradition seems to have died out, or at least become less common in the following centuries, although there is a late third-century portrait of a boy wearing one.

Torcs

From the fourth century AD there was a fashion for torcs. They are commonly shown being worn by slaves and soldiers, and may have been more popular in the eastern part of the Empire, but one or two are shown in the mosaics of Piazza Armerina in Sicily. They were not open at the front in the manner of the Celtic torc, but could be hung with a pendant (**6.1**) or have a large central motif (possibly jewelled; see Justinian's bodyguard, **colour plate 1**).

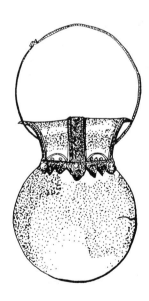

27 Amulet (bulla) *from Pompeii*

Finger-rings

The main item of jewellery worn by men was the finger-ring. During the Republic and the early part of the Empire, the type of ring worn was a status symbol, and laws were passed setting down who could and could not wear them. In the first century Tiberius ruled that the gold ring could only be worn by a third generation freeborn with at least 400,000 *sesterces*, but by the year AD 197, Septimius Severus had extended this honour to all soldiers. Pliny's discussion of the wearing of finger-rings in his *Natural History* says that at first they were worn only on the ring-finger, and then also on the fore-finger, and then on the little finger:

> Gaul and Britain are said to have used the middle finger. At present this is the only finger exempted, while all the others bear the burden, and even each finger-joint has another smaller ring of its own, while others wear only one ring even on that finger, and use it to seal up their signet ring, which is kept stored away as a rarity not deserving the insult of common use (33.6.24-5) (**28.4-5**).

*28 Intaglios and finger-rings.
1 Impression of an intaglio,
possibly from Old Capua,
Lewis collection, Cambridge;
2 Impression of an intaglio,
Caerleon; 3 Moulded paste
intaglio, South Shields
Roman Fort; 4 Hand of
man with finger-rings
holding wreath, painted
linen shroud from Egypt,
Staatliche Kuntsammlungen,
Dresden, Germany; 5 Hand
of young man with finger-
rings holding wreath, painted
linen shroud from Egypt,
Musée du Louvre*

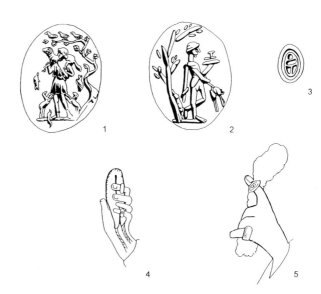

The signet ring was set with an intaglio, a semi-precious stone carved with a small figure or scene, and was part decorative, part amulet and part personal seal. Figures of deities were particularly popular because of the role of the gems as an amulet. When Pliny the Younger sent a nugget of gold in a letter to the Emperor he 'sealed it with [his] signet ring, the chariot-and-four' (*Letters* 10.74.3) so the Emperor could see the letter had not been opened and resealed with some other impression. However, this would not always have been foolproof as hundreds of seals carved with the same motif, such as Fortuna, have been found; there were only so many themes available. The demand for intaglios was such that they were produced in great numbers with competent but not top quality workmanship, and for the poorer end of the market there were cast glass examples with extremely basic motifs (**28.1-3**).

Brooches

Brooches are not strictly speaking jewellery, as they were not purely decorative but essential for fastening cloaks, but they could be exploited for display without the man being considered effeminate. In the first to third centuries, the most common form of brooch depicted in mainstream art is a round disc, usually with a central stone, glass or even cameo setting (**16**). In the fourth century, brooches were of the type now called 'cross-bow,' large inverted cross-shaped brooches that become a symbol of soldiers and civil servants. They were probably not worn by civilians, but they appear frequently in art precisely because it is usually soldiers or civil servants being depicted (**8, 15.1**). As few other fourth century forms of brooches are known, the implication is that almost all civilians used mantles or capes rather than cloaks during this period (**6.3**).

4 Women's clothing

As with the section on men's clothing, each form of garment worn by women will be looked at separately, and the changes in style over time discussed. Many items of women's clothing had the same basic designs as men's clothing, such as the tunic and the mantle, and were only distinguished by size or length. Some items, such as socks, appear to be indistinguishable from male versions and indeed surviving examples can be described as male or female only on the evidence of objects found with them. There were, however, a few garments worn by men but not in the general way used by women, and a few items of distinctively female clothing. The importance of women's clothing as an indicator of social status can be seen in Roman law:

> If any-one accosts young girls who are dressed in the clothes of slaves, his offence will be seen as minor, and even more so if the women are dressed as prostitutes, and not as [respectable] mothers of families. Therefore, if a woman is not dressed as a matron and some-one calls out to her or entices away her attendant, he will not be liable to the action for injury. (*Digest* 47.10.15.15)

In other words, matrons had more protection in law than lower class women, but only if they *looked* respectable.

TUNIC

There were a number of different forms of tunic worn by women, but the study of them is complicated by the fact that portraits of women usually show them respectably dressed in their mantles, large rectangles of enveloping cloth that conceal many of the details of the clothes underneath. The areas most likely to be hidden – the shoulders and arms – are unfortunately those that identify the different forms of tunic. Luckily the mantle is often only shown covering one shoulder, while women shown in indoor scenes do not always wear any outer garment.

The stola
In the late Republic the *stola* was seen as the symbol of female clothing in the same way as the toga was that of male clothing. It could be worn only by matrons (respectable married women) and was worn over the top of the tunic worn by other women. The two distinguishing features of the *stola* that are usually mentioned in first-century literature are its length (it always covered the feet) and a feature called the *institia*. This is still often

1   2   3

29 The stola; *three portrait busts of Antonia the Younger, first century, Vatican Museum, Musée du Louvre and Ny Carlsberg Glyptotek*

described as a 'flounce', but many years ago M. Bieber showed that this is a misunderstanding of the term and of the literary descriptions of the *stola*. As there are no images of a tunic with a flounce round the hem, it was suggested that the *institia* was actually a narrow ribbon that had been painted onto marble statues, since washed away. In fact the *institia* were bands across the shoulders connecting the front and back of the dress, a form of fastening that was Greek in origin and which is found on a number of Hellenistic statues. There were a number of different designs for these shoulder attachments; the simplest were no more than narrow ribbons of cloth, often attached in a position so that there was a loose fold of cloth in between them that sagged down to form a V-shaped neckline (**29**). This V-shaped neckline is an important feature of the *stola*, and on some examples the formation of folds carved in stone sculpture suggest that the neckline was woven (or cut) to form the deep V-shape. Scholtz has made a recent detailed study of the *stola* and has suggested that most bands are two cords across the shoulder, formed by having a loop of cord with the cloth pulled through and sewn over opposite sides of the loop; the junctions were then covered by rectangles of cloth, forming a horizontal band (**colour plate 11**). Unlike the Greek prototype, the *stola* was always worn over a tunic with elbow-length sleeves, and was belted under the breast with a plain cord.

The *stola* came to hold great significance as a symbol of the Roman matron's honour, as it could not be worn by young girls or slaves. However, while the toga continued to have a ceremonial use long after it ceased to be everyday wear, the *stola* was quietly discarded and had fallen out of use probably as early as the late first century. It is sometimes seen on second-century statues, but as it is shown unbelted or belted on the hip, these are likely to be examples of women depicted in historical or mythological costume. The *stola* continued to be used occasionally in literature as a symbol of female modesty for many centuries afterwards, and therefore the term is still widely known, but despite its fame, it was never a long-lived or widespread fashion during the Empire. In Greek, the word was also used of garments worn by men, and the word was

30 Tombstone of couple, showing the woman wearing a gap-sleeved tunic.
    © Soprintendenza Archeologica di Ostia

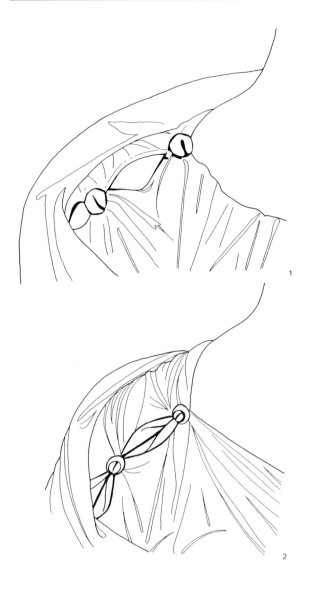

*31 The gap-sleeved tunic, showing details of the fastenings as shown on portrait busts.
1 Faustina II, AD 162-70;
2 Unknown woman, late second century.
Both in the British Museum*

eventually used by the church to describe the long strip of cloth like a scarf worn by priests (the stole), and as such is still in use today.

The tunic
First and second centuries
The gap-sleeved tunic
Republican tombstones of freedwomen are sometimes shown wearing a tunic with sleeves fastened at intervals down the arm. Originally a Greek form of tunic, it was worn by matrons under the *stola* but soon became the outer tunic for upper class Roman women, and is depicted on a huge number of portrait statues and busts. The *stola* could be made from a relatively narrow form of cloth due to the use of bands over the shoulder, while

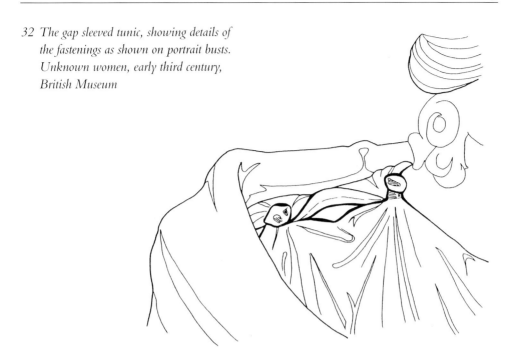

32 The gap sleeved tunic, showing details of the fastenings as shown on portrait busts. Unknown women, early third century, British Museum

the tunic had to be made from a wide piece of cloth that meant that elbow-length sleeves were produced. It was made from two rectangles of cloth sewn together (**3.1**), but instead of the shoulder seam being sewn up as in the male version, it was fastened only at a number of points. The cloth gapes between the fastenings, producing the characteristic appearance of the sleeve (**30, colour plate 12**).

The fastenings are varied in appearance, but are only *c.*1-2cm across, and are usually either upstanding and roughly spherical, or circular and flat. They are generally not perfectly round and often have incisions or indentations on their surface (**31-2**). In the past, they have been assumed to have been metal studs or brooches, but their small size means that they cannot possibly be brooches, and they are not buttons in the modern sense (a disc sewn onto the cloth with a slit in the corresponding opposite cloth edge) as the two edges of cloth touch but do not overlap. They could possibly be discs with a bar or loop on the lower side sewn onto both edges of the cloth, and a bust portrait on the Tomb of the Haterii in Rome showing a fastening in the shape of a small flower could support this view.

An idea of the colour of these fastenings could help in their interpretation, but although this form of tunic appears on many examples of portrait sculpture, there are very few depictions of it from coloured wall paintings, and those that exist are not very helpful. The clearest examples show the fastenings in a pale colour – whatever the colour of the tunic – with darker shadows (**colour plate 13**). These could either represent light reflecting off metal, or could just be a way to make the fastenings more visible. It seems strange that if these fastenings were indeed made of gold or copper alloy they were not more often decorated and treated as an opportunity for display along with other forms of jewellery, and even more strange that they are not shown as smooth circular discs or some other regular shape rather than the uneven shapes found on statues. A possible interpretation is that they are not metal, but cloth; the two edges of the cloth were gathered together (therefore causing the folds seen radiating from each fastening) and a point a centimetre or so below the tip was sewn round and through to fix it in place. The resulting tuft could be left upstanding or could be flattened, but either way it usually had folds within it, as modern experimentation has shown (**colour plates 11-2**). The sagging folds formed by this form of fastenings also helps to produce the gap between the fastenings, which does not happened naturally when the two edges are simply held together without any form of gathering.

There was generally from three to five fastenings on each sleeve, but up to and including seven was not unknown. The last fastening was rarely at the very end of the sleeve, leaving short flaps. Like the *stola*, the tunic was ground-length, and was fastened by a simple cord under the bust.

Short-sleeved tunic

The short-sleeved tunic was made in the same fashion as the male sleeved tunic, but was simply longer in the body. Tombstones show that they were worn by some Republican freedwomen, and the fashion seems to have continued into the first and second centuries for the merchant classes, the poor and therefore also slaves. On some images it could be argued that the short-sleeved tunic is worn belted, but on a number it is clearly unbelted. A wall-painting from Pompeii shows a serving girl in a tavern in an unbelted tunic, as does a relief of the midwife Scribonia Attice from a mid-second-century tomb in Ostia (**33.1**). The musician and some of the mourners on a relief from the late first- or early second-century Tomb of the Haterii from Rome also wear unbelted short-sleeved tunics (**33.2**). The tunics of the serving girl from Pompeii and Scribonia's assistant are calf-length, which is probably a distinction of class, as shorter tunics required less cloth (much stress for example was put on the fact that the *stola* of the upper-class matron covered her feet).

Colour

Both the Greeks and Etruscans, who influenced Roman costume, loved patterns, borders and bright colours, and in the second century BC Plautus mentions the bordered gown, the royal or the exotic, and the feather patterned in a list of different tunic types (*Epidicus* 2.2.228-34). In the late first century BC and the early first century AD there are references to *segmentata*, which were bands of patterned decoration, which might be the broad bands round the hem of tunics as shown in colour plate **13**.

Female costume during the first few centuries of the Empire appears to make much less use of borders and pattern, but this may result purely from the bias of the surviving evidence. The most common forms of decoration were simple stripes of colour, usually two narrow stripes down the front and back of the tunic. Ovid recommends purple stripes for a pale woman (*Art of Love* 3.270), and a portrait of a woman from Pompeii has a dark brown stripe on a red-brown tunic. Portraits from Egypt show tunics with two dark stripes down the front, such as red on green and black on purple (**colour plate 14**). While linens

*33 Unbelted short-sleeved tunics of the first and second centuries. 1 Midwife Scribonia Attice and
assistant, second-century bas relief, Ostia, Italy; 2 Musician at funeral, bas relief from the Tomb
of the Haterii, Vatican Museum*

and silks would only have pastel colours, wool could provide vivid colours: Ovid
mentions woollen clothes, presumably tunics, with borders, in purple, sky-blue, water-
coloured, saffron, green, amethyst, white, chestnut, almond and wax-yellow (*Art of Love*
3.169-88).

Third and fourth century
The short-sleeved tunic

The gap-sleeved tunic continued into the late third century on the evidence of portrait
busts. Sometimes this can be explained as examples of Imperial women wearing
'traditional' clothing or of a new head being put on a pre-existing statue wearing the old
style of tunic, but there are a few examples where this is clearly not the case, such as the
Annona sarcophagus portrait dated to the late third century (**9.1**). This is a betrothal or
marriage scene, unusual in that not only is the woman not wearing a bridal mantle as was
usual in such scenes, but that her tunic is slipping down her shoulder in an way not seen
elsewhere with the gap-sleeve tunic. Usually the bare shoulder is the reserve of goddesses
or women dressed as goddesses in tube-dresses fastened by a single brooch at the
shoulder, so the exact interpretation of this scene is therefore not fully understood.

A new form of tunic did develop, however, from the early third century. The reliefs on
the Arch of Severus in Lepcis Magna dated AD 203-4 show the Empress Julia Domna
wearing the gap-sleeved tunic in one scene and a tunic with fully-sewn sleeves in another

34 *Short-sleeved tunics of the third century. 1 Julia Domna, bas relief from the Arch of Septimius Severus, Lepcis Magna, AD 203; 2 Unknown woman, early third-century bust, Museo Archeologico Nazionale Napoli, Italy*

35 *Christian women at prayer, wearing unbelted tunics. 1 Late third-century wall painting from the Catacombs of Priscilla, Rome; 2 early fourth-century wall painting from the Catacomb of Traso, Rome; 3 early fourth-century wall painting from the Catacomb of the Giordani, Rome*

(**34.1**). A bust dated to the early third century has a similar short-sleeve tunic, probably with striped decoration (**34.2**). This is of course the same type of short-sleeved tunic worn in the first and second centuries, but it is belted under the bust and is long enough to cover the feet, and was now being worn by the higher classes.

The long-sleeved tunic

Sometime during the third century a new style of female tunic came into fashion, presumably at the same time as the new long-sleeved form of male tunic (see p33). This tunic was called a *dalmaticus*. Although mentioned as early as the second century, it only seems to be in the late third or very early fourth century that it became widespread as a fashion. In the fourth century there are numerous depictions of women wearing this new fashion, although as it happens, most of these are of Christians and not of the upper social classes. The dalmatic is a T-shaped tunic with proper sleeves, usually reasonably wide, decorated with two stripes up front and back and round the lower edge of the sleeves. It often had a curved lower edge, and could be fringed.

There are two particularly important elements to this costume which distinguish it from previous fashions; it was worn unbelted and it could also be relatively short so that for the first time respectable women were showing their ankles in public (**35, colour plate 15**). It is unfortunately not known exactly when this new style came in, who introduced it, or even if it was accepted by all sections of society, as it was so different from what had gone before.

The late third- or early fourth-century catacombs in Rome show a number of Christian women wearing this style of tunic. Most show women in pale coloured dalmatics with dark coloured stripes, although the reverse is occasionally known. Usually

36 Tunic decorations from Egypt in purple and white, California Academy of Sciences. 1 Fifth-century tunic fragment; 2 Fourth-century tunic fragment

37   Late forms of tunics, mid-fourth-century reliefs in silver from the Proiecta Casket, British Museum. 1 Proiecta being escorted to the baths; 2 Proiecta dressing her hair

the stripes are plain, but a picture from the Cemetery of Priscilla and one from the Cemetery of Traso both show stripes with a decorative pattern (both women have hairstyles of the type fashionable *c*.AD 270-310; **35**). Figure **36** shows two styles of decorated tunic stripes with dark and pale backgrounds. These are both from male tunics, but they give an idea of some of the simpler patterns. Although women occasionally have decorated stripes, they are never shown during this period with the roundels used on the male tunics of the same period.

There are a number of depictions in the Catacombs under the Via Latina, the decoration of which has been dated to AD 320-50. There are at least two depictions of praying women in pale coloured short tunics decorated with dark stripes and one of a praying woman wearing a ground-length version. It is not clear if the length of the dress is due to personal preference, age or wealth, but it is perhaps most likely that it was a matter of wealth. A mosaic at Piazza Armerina Villa that is probably nearly contemporary with the Catacomb paintings (*c*.AD 300-350) shows the mistress of the house on the way to the baths in the company of her sons and two female slaves (**colour plate 8**). The mistress wears an ankle-length striped dress with very wide sleeves while the two slaves wear mid-calf length tunics. The tunic of the mistress may possibly be belted under the bust, but it is possible she is in fact wearing a mantle draped round her neck with both ends hanging down her back (a fashion seen more clearly on the mistress on the Proiecta Casket, **37.1**). One of the servants, however, quite clearly does have her tunic belted under her bust, pulling in her full sleeves at the same time. Some of the slaves on the Proiecta Casket also wear their tunic belted, as does a slave in the tomb-paintings of a grave in Silistra (dated to the late fourth century). Both sets of slaves have tied in their long sleeves as with the Piazza Armerina slave, producing long loops like wings (**38**). It is likely that during this period slaves or those who had to work wore their tunics belted at times to keep their full skirts and sleeves out of the way, while the rich had no such need.

38 Slaves with belted tunics. 1 Mid-fourth-century relief in silver, Proiecta Casket, British Museum; 2 Fourth-century tomb wall painting, Silistra, Bulgaria

Colour

The same wide range of colours current in the first and second centuries was also used in the third and fourth centuries. The long-sleeved tunics could be either pale or dark coloured, although the decorated stripes were almost all purple and white. The mistress from Piazza Armerina is shown in a tunic of pink with broad dark brown and white stripes down the front of the gown, and round the lower part of the sleeves. The slaves accompanying her also have stripes on their tunics, although theirs are much narrower; one has a yellow tunic with red and black stripes, and the other a dark pink tunic with brown stripes.

Late fourth century

The Proiecta casket, dated roughly to the period AD 330-370, shows the mistress – Proiecta herself – in three different costumes. The portrait bust shows her with a tunic with an all-over pattern of dots belted high under the bust with long, tight-fitting sleeves (**15.1**). In the procession to the bath-house she wears a full-length gown with wide sleeves, but it is not clear if it is belted as she has a mantle draped round her neck (**37.1**). In the final scene, Proiecta is sitting in a chair doing her hair, wearing an inner tunic with

39 Serena and her son Eucharius, late fourth-century ivory diptych.
© Monza Cathedral Treasury

long tight-fitting sleeves and a sleeveless overtunic (**37.2**). It is possible this overgown should be belted, as shown in the portrait scene, but Proiecta is otherwise fully dressed, including jewellery.

The fashion for two tunics can be seen more clearly on the portrait of Serena (*c*.AD 400). She has an inner tunic with long, tight-fitting sleeves, with a wider tunic over the top, tied under the bust with a jewelled belt (**39**). This fashion of tight-sleeved inner tunic and looser outer tunic mimics that of fourth-century men (**10.6**). The tunic is not only once again belted but ground-length, which fits in with the general late antique trend for women to be almost completely covered.

Fifth to sixth century

The details of the tunics of the women of the court of Theodora are not fully clear because of the short mantles they are wearing, but they appear to have long, tight-fitting sleeves, and a couple of contemporary scenes of Christian stories suggest that the fashion for a long-sleeved inner tunic and short-sleeved outer tunic still held sway. These women could of course be shown in 'old-fashioned' clothes as they are characters in Biblical stories, but their head coverings are very similar to those worn by Theodora's court, suggesting that their dress is also contemporary.

The Biblical characters have simple striped tunics, but the court women have more elaborate dresses with decorated stripes, or a border round the lower edge or even roundels, previously seen only on male tunics (**colour plate 2**). All of them wear tunics woven with an all-over pattern, including geometrical patterns, plant motifs and birds. This reflects the taste, imported from the East, for the ornate, the colourful and the bejewelled in the late Empire. Theodora herself wears a very different costume, based on male military dress, that stresses her status as someone separate from the women of even the highest class who make up her court.

Colour

Most women wore tunics in one colour with stripes down front and back. The rich used cloth with all-over patterns; for example, the ladies of Theodora's court wore tunics with a geometric pattern, blue birds against a pale pink ground, red birds against green, and a foliage pattern. As well as patterned cloth, some of the tunics have decorated stripes, roundels, and a large border round the hem.

Undertunics

Various ancient authors use a number of terms for clothing which apparently refer to some type of undertunic. In the Republic, some women wearing short-sleeved tunics are shown clearly wearing an undertunic, visible at the neck, but it is clear that undertunics were not usually worn with the gap-sleeved tunic, as they would otherwise be seen in the gap between the fastenings. Undertunics are sometimes seen with the long-sleeved tunics (**35.3**), but even then they were still not universal. In the sixth century there is possibly evidence that an undertunic was also sometimes worn, although the evidence comes from figures in Biblical scenes. Two ladies from a mosaic in the Basilica of St Apollinare Nuovo in Ravenna wear long-sleeved tunics and mantles in blue and brown, with white caps on their heads and a white undertunic visible at the neck. A sixth-century illuminated manuscript (the *Vienna Genesis*) shows a woman – the biblical Rebecca – wearing a pink inner tunic and pink outer tunic (of contemporary fashion), with a glimpse of a white undertunic decorated with a black pattern along its hem. It is clear that throughout the Roman period undertunics were sometimes worn, but in what circumstances is not known.

Belts

Roman women always tied their tunics high under the bust rather than at the waist. Depictions of women wearing their tunic belted at the waist or hips are likely to be of goddesses, their priestesses, mythological figures or figures copied from Hellenistic models. In the first to third centuries belts were no more than twisted cord, tied in a reef knot with only short ends hanging down (**34.1**), in general probably of a contrasting colour to the tunic. The rich freedwoman Fortunata wore a 'yellow-green small belt' over a cherry-coloured tunic (Petronius, *Saty.* 67.4) while the slave Fotis wore a reddish band over a linen tunic (Apuleius, *Ass* 11.7) .

40 Tunic with ornamented belt, painted linen shroud from Egypt. Musée du Louvre

In the late third and fourth century, the belt, when worn, was still often no more than a cord (**colour plate 8**). There was, however, a growing fashion for elaboration as can be seen on a painted shroud from Egypt showing a woman in a purple tunic wearing a belt of red cloth fastened at the front by a large circular central gem set in gold. This could perhaps be a brooch, or the gem and its setting could have had a bar across the back that the cloth was tied onto; either way, the two narrow ends of the belt hang below the fastening (**40**). A fourth-century fragment of cloth, now in Berlin, shows a woman in a purple tunic with yellow stripes wearing a thin, pale red belt fastened with a large oval dark blue or black stone set in gold.

When two tunics became fashionable, by the end of the fourth century, the tie became a proper belt, probably made out of leather. Serena wears one with a central rectangular plate set with an oval stone on a belt decorated with further jewels (**39**). A fifth-century wall painting from the Catacombs of St January in Naples shows a young girl in a cream-spotted red tunic, with a decorated belt with one very large central blue or black gem with further gold-set gems and pearls to either side.

The hips or the waist are a more natural place to fasten a dress than under the bust as then the hips and buttocks stop the belt slipping down any further. Under the bust, however, unless a woman is pregnant, there is nothing to stop the belt sliding down the ribs. There is no evidence of the belt being threaded through loops on the tunic, so it is possible it was pinned or sewn onto the dress at intervals to keep it in place.

Dining-clothes

Women changed into a different set of clothes for eating in company in the same way as men (see p39). The dining-clothes consisted of tunic and mantle, which may possibly have been of the same colour; Martial refers to a man giving his mistress a gift of 'leek green dining-clothes' instead of buying a toga for himself (*Ep.* 10.29). The *Digest*, a series of questions and answers on legal queries, also mentions female dining-clothes. In this case a woman called Sempronia Pia had been left Tabian mantles and three tunics with small mantles *(palliola)* which she was allowed to pick out herself. The question seems to be whether she could only pick the clothes from the individual tunics and mantles of the deceased woman, or if she could choose them from sets of dining-clothes, with the implication that there was some distinction in value between the two (*Digest* 34.38.1).

MANTLE, CLOAK AND CAPE

Mantle

Male and female outer garments had originally been very similar, consisting of long lengths of cloth draped round the body, but while the male version was transformed into the toga, the female version remained very much the same throughout the Roman period. The *palla* was a large rectangle of cloth, without the curved lower edge of the toga, that covered the body from shoulder to knee or lower calf. It had presumably once been intended as protection against bad weather or the cold, but it soon became a necessary covering for a modest woman, and no respectable woman would leave her house without her head covered and her body concealed by it. The mantle, like the toga, needed at least one hand to keep it in place. A cloak fastened on the shoulder by a brooch allows both hands to remain free, but only in very rare circumstances did women wear a cloak (see below). The *palla* was therefore no more suitable for working in than the developed forms of the toga, and while that was not a problem for the rich who had slaves to carry objects for them, it would have been cumbersome for the majority of the population. In the first century there are a number of depictions of women with their mantles tied in a great knot on their hips to keep their hands free, but these are usually religious scenes with the women playing musical instruments or making offerings, which may be based on Hellenistic prototypes, and it may not have been an everyday method of wearing the mantle.

In the Republican period, the mantle was not so very different to the toga (cf **41.1** and **10.1**), and while there were a number of different ways of draping it, it stayed the same basic shape and never developed the complexities of the toga. One end was draped over the left shoulder and then brought round the back where it could either be brought over the right shoulder, concealing most of the figure, or it was brought under the right arm. It was then flung over the left shoulder or draped over the arm (**41**).

In the first century there were complaints about how the voluminous mantles shrouded women and hid them from view. While the large mantle seems to have continued throughout the Roman period, there was a general tendency towards a smaller and less all-enveloping form. The wall-paintings in the catacombs of Rome never show a mantle being worn with the fourth-century short tunic. The Egyptian portraits, however, sometimes show a mantle being worn either like a shawl over both shoulders, or with one end hanging down over the right shoulder, and the rest brought round the back and under the right arm and then across the body to the lower left arm (rather than back over the shoulder). The mantle across the front of the body is often shown draped in a curve (**colour plate 15**). From the third century some mantles have added decoration such as roundels, L- and H-shapes, as with the male mantles (**42**).

The mantle shown with the fourth-century full-length tunic is much narrower than the earlier form. It was worn so that there was no visible cloth hanging down the front; either the end that usually hung down the front of the body was very short and hidden under the drapery above it, or both ends were thrown back over the shoulders; either way, the shoulders and upper arms were covered by an arc of cloth. Proiecta is shown wearing her mantle in this way, and so perhaps is the mistress of Piazza Armerina (**colour plate 8; 37.1**).

Also during the fourth century, and just possibly the third, there was a fashion for a new form of mantle with wide decorated borders such as that worn by the daughter on the gold and glass portrait from Brescia (**colour plate 16**). There are least two other depictions of similar mantles with stiff borders decorated with elements such as circles, diamonds and tendrils, but none of these portraits is full-length and the exact form of the mantle is unclear. The gold and glass portrait also shows an unusual method of wearing a mantle: the mother wears hers tied in a knot on the breast. This is shown on a few other gold and glass portraits, which show that it is not an 'Isis knot' worn by priestesses (see p12).

The small mantle continued into the fifth century and beyond. That worn by Serena is rolled heavily at the top and is no more than knee length (**39**), while the women of the court of Theodora wear ones that are no more than shawls (**colour plate 2**). Here they are worn with one end hanging down the left side, with the other end taken round the back, over the right shoulder and thrown back over the left shoulder again.

Colour

Frequently the mantle was the same colour as the tunic underneath, suggesting the concept of a set of clothing, presumably bought or made at the same time (cf **colour plate 14**). It could, however, also be in a contrasting colour, and could be either darker or lighter than the tunic; portraits from Egypt show purple with a white tunic, white with a dark blue tunic and orange with a green tunic. Third- and fourth-century mantles sometimes had purple and white roundels, while fifth-century examples could be patterned. The mantles of the ladies of Theodora's court are in a mixture of colours; white with an overall brown geometric pattern and gold roundels; plain white with gold roundels; orange with blue dots in sets of three; gold with an all-over pattern of green crosses imposed on red circles, and gold with blue and black crosses or stars (**colour plate 2**).

41 Women wearing the mantle. 1 Statue of unknown woman and daughter, c.50 BC, Palazzo dei Conservatori, Rome; 2 Second-century statue of Vestal Virgin, Museo Nazionale, Rome; 3 unknown woman, late second-century statue, Museo Capitolino, Rome

Other mantles

Small versions of the *palla* were also used *(palliola;* see p87). Other forms of mantle were called *amictus, amiculum* and *amictorium*, meaning garments thrown on or around a person; these may well simply be generic terms for a wrap rather than being distinct forms of mantle. Women could also use the *endromis*, the thick mantle worn by athletes, as shown by one of the exercising ladies from the Piazza Armerina mosaic.

Capes

Although women are very rarely shown wearing capes, it is clear from the literary evidence that they could do so when travelling, and presumably during bad weather. Claudius' wife Messalina also wore a shoulder cape *(cucullus)*, creeping at night 'wearing a night cape and attended by no more than a single maid' (Juvenal 6.118) while Diocletian's Edict refers to capes *(caracallae)* of coarse linen for the use of women of the lower classes. The Edict also refers to linen 'hoods' *(mafortia)* worn by women, but as they are listed as being dyed with

42 Decorated mantle, fourth-century painted linen and plaster mask from Egypt, Royal Museum of Scotland

purple, they are likely to have been more fashion items than purely functional, and it is perhaps more likely that they were simply shawls, a narrow form of mantle that was worn round the shoulders and over the head. The early fourth-century writer Nonius Marcellus equates the *mafortium* with the earlier *ricinium* or head veil, and calls it a woman's short small mantle (Nonius 14). One of these 'hoods' in the Edict is described as having vertical stripes made using one pound of purple and costing 55,000 *denarii*, one of the most expensive garments listed in the Edict.

Cloaks

Women did not, on the whole, wear cloaks. Some priestesses fastened their mantles with a brooch, but they did not wear them in the manner of men's cloaks, covering both shoulders and fastened on the right side. Instead the cloth was looped under one arm and fastened on the opposite shoulder (cf **55.4**). Poppaea, Nero's mother, had a general's cloak made for her, and Theodora is shown wearing a man's cloak (**colour plate 2**), but both are Imperial women and are 'honorary men' because of their position.

Togas

In the first century there are a number of literary references to prostitutes wearing the toga. Martial, for example, suggests that a toga would make a more suitable gift for a notorious adulteress than expensive scarlet and violet clothes (*Ep.* 2.39), and Horace contrasts a 'toga'd maid' with an honourable matron (*Sat.* 1.1.62-3). There seems to be no evidence that prostitutes *had* to wear the toga, only that they were the only women who could. It is not clear why they wore it, or why they would want to; the first-century toga was even more cumbersome and concealing than the *palla* worn by respectable women. Perhaps the prostitute's version of a toga was smaller and lighter, or more akin to the Republican toga, but it seems unlikely that a profession more used to wearing transparent Coan silk would take kindly to the toga.

UNDERWEAR

The extent to which underwear was regularly worn is not clear for while bras and briefs are known from images of athletes, acrobats, and prostitutes, they are functional outerware rather than underwear. Nevertheless, the bra seems to have been an accepted part of female underwear, although there is less evidence for briefs. Cicero's description of P. Clodius dressed as a woman in the first century BC lists the clothes he wore, and on two different occasions mentions both breastband and leg coverings, but not briefs (*Soothsayers* 43-4; *Clodius* 15.21-4). Ovid mentions both the breastband and leg coverings as hiding places for love letters (*Art of Love* 3.621-4), while Martial's description of Lesbia's tunic catching between her buttocks would also suggest that no briefs were being worn (*Ep.* 11.99.1-5). When Lucius' lover in *The Golden Ass* undressed he says 'without delay she stripped off her clothes, even down to the band that bound up her breasts' (10.21) without mentioning the removal of any briefs, and a woman shown in the process of taking off her tunic on a silver bucket in Naples Museum has no briefs on underneath. On the other hand, it is highly likely that women wore some form of briefs for the duration of their periods.

Breastband

The breastband was a long length of cloth or leather wrapped round the breasts with the end tucked in; the statue of Venus and a mosaic of a nymph from France show them wrapping or unwrapping their breastbands (**43, 44.1**). In the late Republic the word for breastband was *strophium*, but by the first century AD the term *fascia* (or *fascea*) had become more common. The word simply means strip of cloth or bandage, and it could be used of bands of cloth used for any purpose, including lower leg coverings.

   The breastband is often found on depictions of mythological women connected with love or sex, such as Venus and nymphs, as well as human lovers and prostitutes at work. While it is not surprising that the prostitutes are not wearing briefs, the mythological women are also otherwise naked, or simply have a mantle draped round their hips, suggesting that the combination of bra and briefs was not the usual 'set' of underwear as it is nowadays.

   Experiments by members of the re-enactment group Quinta have shown that to stay up the cloth needs to be as much as five metres long so that it can be firmly wrapped round the breasts six or seven times. Breastbands of a shorter length have a tendency to slip down, even when walking, let alone taking part in energetic activities such as athletic exercises. The length of the breastband may possibly be indicated by a reference in the

43 Statuette of Venus unwrapping her breastband.
© Museum Burg Linn, Germany

Scriptores Historiae Augustae to the birth of Clodius Albinus, where a bandage was long enough to wrap a baby in:

> It was customary in his family that the bandages in which the children are wrapped should be of a reddish colour. In his case, however, it chanced that the bandages which had been prepared by his mother during her pregnancy had been washed and were not yet dry, and he was therefore wrapped in a breastband (*fascea*) of his mother's, and this, as it happened, was purple. (SHA *Clodius Albinus* 5.9)

The word *fascea* could of course refer to other forms of bandage, as noted above.

Martial's gift tag for a breastband suggests that it could be used to produce a bit of cleavage: 'band, compress my lady's swelling breasts, so that my hand may find something to clasp and cover' (*Ep.* 14.134), but generally the breastband squashes and flattens the breast. Ovid in fact suggests that the sight of a large-breasted woman unrestrained by a breastband would cure a man of love (*Remedies* 338). Of course, for some women, flattening the breast is the last thing they want to do. There are a number of depictions – generally of mythological women – where it is clear that the breastband is wrapped round *under* the breasts; assuming this is not simply a Hellenistic convention, it may be that the band was used in this way to give a little uplift to the bust (**44.2**).

Briefs

Briefs were worn by women in the bathhouse. Before having a bath, the Romans liked to work up a good sweat, and depictions of female 'athletes' all come from bathhouses, where women could exercise in relative privacy. Martial mentions a woman playing ball games wearing briefs, and another woman being modest wearing briefs while in the bathhouse (*Ep.* 7.67; 3.87), although it is not clear if the briefs were also worn in the water. The briefs could be worn alone, or in conjunction with a breastband. The mosaic from the family bathhouse at Piazza Armerina shows ten women exercising, eight of them in bikinis, holding, amongst other things, the palm leaf and wreath of a winner, suggesting the games were in earnest (**colour plate 18**). Although some of the bikinis are all red, others have green or blue breastbands with the red briefs. The briefs are not tied at the sides, and it is not clear how they stay up without ties or any form of elastic, unless they are extremely tight.

Other images show the briefs being worn by themselves. Stucco reliefs of women from a third-century private bath-suite in Carthage show four women wearing small black openwork briefs tied at the sides, with the ends dangling down to mid-thigh or below (**44.3**). A very similar garment has survived in waterlogged conditions in London. It is made out of leather in an hour-glass shape, with integral ties on both sides, and an openwork design on the front. A second example from London, without any openwork decoration but also of leather, was found in a first-century context (**colour plate 17**). Both pairs are very small, and C. van Driel-Murray has suggested they were worn by child acrobats.

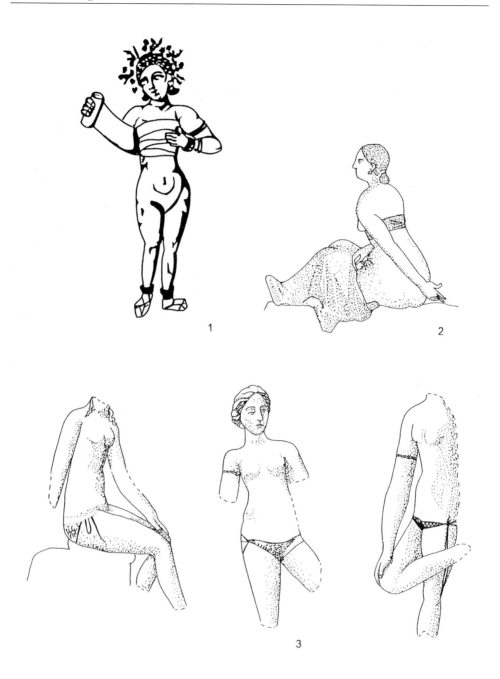

44 *Breastbands and briefs. 1 Female entertainer, fourth-century mosaic, Hippo Regius, Algeria; 2 Woman in bed, first-century wall painting from Pompeii; 3 Stucco reliefs of three women from a private bath-house in Dougga, Tunisia, possibly third-century*

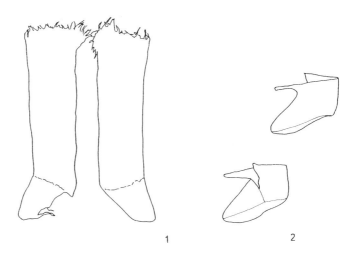

45 Woollen knee and ankle socks from a second-century grave at Les Martres-de-Veyre, France

1   2

Leggings

Statues of the first and second centuries usually show upper-class women in sandals without any form of sock, but it is clear that women would wear some form of puttee on occasion. The word used is *fascia* or *fasciola* (little strip/bandage), suggesting some form of puttee, or piece of cloth folded round the foot in the modern Russian manner. Cicero refers to a 'woman's house-shoes and purple puttees' (*fasceolis*; *Soothsayers* 21.44), and Ovid might be referring to puttees when he recommended that 'lean ankles should never be released from their bonds' when referring to ways a woman could make herself attractive (*Art of Love* 3.271-2).

Women also wore proper ankle-length socks. The word for sock, *soccus*, is also taken to mean 'slipper' (as well as being the traditional footwear of a comic actor) and it is sometimes difficult to tell which is meant. Catullus mentions flame-coloured *socci* worn by a bride (61.8-10) while Diocletian's Edict refers to purple, white and gilded *socci* in the section on footwear, although without identifying them as either male or female items of dress (18-23). Pliny may well be referring to socks when he refers to women fixing pearls 'not only to the straps of their sandals but all over their little *socci*' (*Nat. Hist.* 9.56.114). A third-century painted shroud from Egypt shows a woman wearing socks with her sandals; dressed in a calf-length white tunic and mantle she has bright red socks with her sandals (**colour plate 15**). The second-century graves from Les Martres-de-Veyre in France also produced a pair of ankle socks, as well as a pair of knee-high stockings (**45**). The long socks, like the ankle socks, were made of pieces of shaped woollen cloth sewn together, and would have had a narrow cord laced through the top of them, below the fringe, to act as garters. The ankle socks have a strap to cross the front of the foot, but there is no surviving method of fastening them. It is unfortunately not clear how often such long socks were worn, or if short and long socks were worn according to the season, or if the fashion for long socks were restricted to the north-west provinces, as the evidence in art is concealed under long tunics. Full length trousers or hose, however, were quite firmly the preserve of the man.

From the late third century enclosed shoes or ankle boots came into fashion, and there is a lack of evidence for leg coverings. It is unlikely, however, that either the need for socks or their design changed much.

HAIRSTYLES AND HATS

Hats were rarely worn by women in Italy, and instead they wore their hair in elaborate hairstyles. These hairstyles changed so frequently during the Empire they can be used to date statues or other artwork. The main evidence for the developing hairstyles, at least as worn by Imperial women, is their portraits on coins. There are some drawbacks, however: the coins of the women cannot usually be dated as closely as the coins of the Emperors, and often they were issued posthumously, so that is not clear whether the hairstyle is the one used in life or simply the current style. There are also some reigns when no coins were issued with female portraits, or the women are shown with the mantle over their heads, and there are some hairstyles known to have been worn by women that are not shown on coins at all.

Although there were frequent changes in the styles, they occurred over five centuries or more. Some styles could last for 20 or 30 years so it was quite possible for some women to wear the same hairstyle most of their adult life. Only a few of the Imperial women are shown with more than one hairstyle, and it is likely that new fashions were introduced by a new Empress to distinguish herself from her predecessor. Women wishing to be fashionable, wherever they lived in the Empire, could use the official statues and coin portraits to follow the latest hairstyles from the Imperial court.

Coin portraits are almost exclusively side views. More details of the hairstyles, including front and back, can be obtained from portrait busts and statues. These often show the hair in great detail, including numerous intricately carved small plaits, and yet they never show any of the hairpins that must have kept the hair in place. It is possible to push the pins in far enough to hide the heads, but pins with pearls, beads or ornately carved heads were clearly meant to be seen. The stone portraits also rarely depict necklaces or earrings, so it is presumably simply a convention of portrait art not to show these details.

Many of the hairstyles required false hair or pads, and literary sources also mention the use of wigs. Many of these hairstyles are very complex and would only have been for the rich and leisured classes; the poor women would have had much simpler styles. All adult women would have had long hair, the only exceptions being women who habitually wore wigs, slaves who had had their own hair cut off to provide the hair for such wigs, and possibly some priestesses, as well as women who had been ill. Women would not have appeared in public with short hair from choice. The hair was always worn pinned up, unless the woman wanted to show distress by not taking care of her appearance, such as at funerals.

c.40 BC – c.AD 14
The hairstyle of Livia (wife of Augustus) consisted of a strip of hair on the top of the head brushed forward over the forehead and then folded back forming a knot (*nodus*) at the front, held in place by a tie or pin. The strip of hair then crossed the top of the head in a

*46 Hairstyles of the first and second centuries. 1 40 BC – AD 14; 2 AD 14–37; 3 AD 38–64;
4 AD 64–8; 5 AD 80–98; 6–8 AD 98–138*

band, while the hair round the face was waved and lightly twisted towards a low bun usually made up of a thick plait or plaits, with a plait wrapped round its base (**46.1**).

c.AD 14 – c.AD 37

The *nodus* went out of fashion, but the waved band of hair round the face and the low bun of plaits bound round with another plait continued (**46.2**).

c.AD 38 – c.AD 64

Agrippina I (mother of Caligula) modified this style; the waved band round the face was now flat on the top before breaking out in a bank of short curls on either side before being rolled in a loose band to join the bun at the nape of the neck. This had now become elongated so that the loops of plaits hung down the back of the neck, although it was still bound round at the top. There was often a single ringlet on either side behind the ears (**46.3**). Agrippina II (third wife of Claudius) was portrayed with a very similar style, although she was usually shown on coins with two ringlets.

c.AD 64 – c.AD 68

Poppaea Sabina (second wife of Nero) had almost the same style, but now the bank of curls was much wider, extending back over half the head (**46.4**).

c.AD69 – c.AD79

Vespasian's wife and daughter had died before he became Emperor so no official statues or coin issued were produced. It is likely that the hairstyles in this period were closer to the following rather than the proceeding styles, as people would not have wanted to associate themselves with the disgraced Imperial family of Nero and the rival Emperors of the civil war.

c.AD 80 – c.AD 98

Coins of both Julia Titi (daughter of Titus) and Domitia (wife of Domitian: coins of AD 82-3) show them with two different hairstyles. Both styles had a wedge-shaped raised bank of tight curls in a crescent from ear to ear. One style then had the hair pulled back in numerous small, separate plaits that again hung in long loops at the nape of the neck, loosely tied with other small plaits (**46.5**). The second style had the plaits drawn up into a large plump bun or coil of plaits near the top of the back of the head.

c.AD 98 – c.AD 138

Although Plotina (wife of Trajan) became Empress in AD 98, no coins depicting her were produced until AD 112, when she is shown with a hairstyle developed from the previous style. Round her face was a narrow band of false hair, downturned in front of her ears, marked out with C-shaped waves while above it her hair was brushed over a raised pad to form a peak. The hair was then divided into numerous small plaits drawn down to the nape of her neck, where they hung in long loops, as in the previous century (**46.6**). At the same time, on coins the deceased Matidia (Trajan's sister) and her daughter Marciana are shown with a different style: there was the same narrow band of hair and the peak (or often two or three peaks of hair), but behind them the small plaits are twisted up into an open circle. From the side, this open circle is often slightly twisted, forming almost a Z-shape lying on its side (**46.7**). The second hairstyle worn by Matidia and Sabina probably developed into one of the best known of Roman hairstyles (but one that is not depicted on coins), where the bank of curls grows extremely tall. From the front, the bank of curls started out being wider than it was tall, but gradually developed until it was taller than it was wide (**46.8**). Sabina (Hadrian's wife) wore the same style as Matidia and Marciana, and another, simpler style, closer to Plotina's style: her loose, plain hair is drawn up over a pad, and pulled back in a loose ponytail at the back of her neck, with the ends folded under and tied rather low down towards the end of the tail. A ribbon runs from in front of the pad to tie at the back of the head (**47.9**).

c.AD 138 – c.AD 146

Faustina I (wife of Antoninus Pius) died in AD 141, so most of her coins are posthumous, but they again show that the Empress chose a new hairstyle that was very distinct from that which had gone before. Her hair was parted in the centre, and set in soft waves round the head to the back where the hair was divided into a number of plaits which were then loosely twisted together up the back of her head and then coiled into a neat, flat bun right on the top of the head (**47.10-1; 30; colour plate 19**). On some statues the bun grows much taller and becomes almost conical in shape.

c.AD 146 – c.AD 160

Faustina II (Faustina I's daughter and wife of Marcus Aurelius) had a hairstyle different from her mother's. The hair round her face was divided up to form long overlapping curls pulled back away from her head, sometimes to a braid worn like a headband. The rest of her hair was divided into sections that were lightly rolled before being pulled to the back of her head where they were coiled into a flat open bun made up of plaits. A distinctive element of the bun were the ends of a number of plaits that came from under it, their ends tucked back into its centre (**47.12, colour plate 19**).

c.AD 161 – c.AD 180

When she grew older, Faustina adopted a new hairstyle. It grew more bulky, with more body, and was set in waves before being pulled back to a large round bun low at the back of her neck, sometimes shown as coiled plaits but sometimes as a looser bun with an interlaced design on statues. Sometimes the hair round the face is shown twisted or plaited before it feeds into the bun. Faustina's daughter Lucilla is shown with the same hairstyles (**47.13; colour plate 19**).

c.AD 180 – c.AD 200

Crispina (wife of Commodus) is shown wearing the same style as the elder Faustina II and Lucilla, but in some of her coin portraits, the style has developed further. The hair was still heavily waved, but now fully covered the ears before being drawn back to the bun, which was now much larger, reaching almost to the top of the head. The wife and daughter of Didius Julianus (reigned for one year, AD 193) have the same large bun. Marble statues show quite clearly that these buns were false pieces with elaborate interlacing star patterns (**47.14**). The early coins of Julia Domna (wife of Septimius Severus) show her with the same huge bun, although the hair round her face droops down onto her neck before being brought up to the bun. Julia Domna's hairstyles were always very large: other women copied the style, but usually without the same bulk.

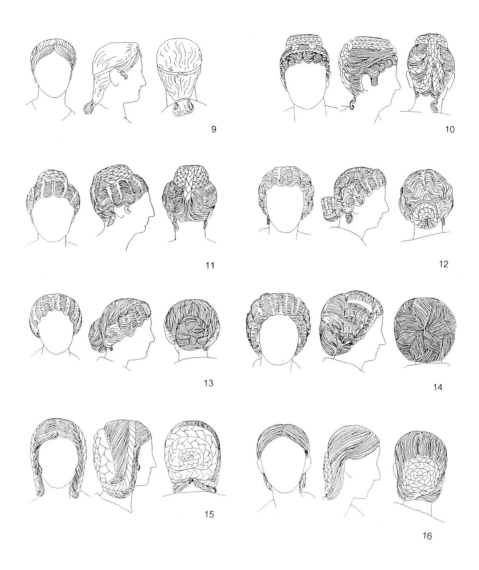

*47 Hairstyles of the second and third centuries. 9 AD 98–138; 10–1 AD 138–46;
12 AD 146–60; 13 AD 161–80; 14 AD 180–200 15–6 AD 200–17*

c.AD 200 – AD 217

Julia Domna's second hairstyle was equally large. The hair was still heavily waved, and the hair round the face was often twisted into a cable pattern before being drawn back to the bun (**47.15**). The bun could be large, covering the whole of the back of the head, in a single spiralled plait, or it could be low and oval, at the nape of the neck. Plautilla (wife of Caracalla, AD 202-5) is shown with this second style, her hair not as bulky but still covering her ears and heavily waved, with a low spiral plaited bun (**47.16**). She is also shown with a very different style, with her hair divided into sections and twisted in rows before being pulled back to a flat bun at the back of her head.

c.AD 218 – c.AD 240

Julia Maesa (grandmother of Elagabalus) is shown with her straight hair covering her ears and pulled back to a spiralled bun covering the back of her head, but her hair did not hang down so low on her shoulders, nor did her bun cover as much of her head as Julia Domna's bulky styles. Coins also show her with waved hair and a small, oval bun made of a spiralled plait at the nape of her neck. This low, very small oval bun style, now with the hair tucked behind the ears, is worn by all of Elagabalus' wives, Severus Alexander's wife and his mother, Julia Mamaea (although Elagabalus' first wife Julia Paula is also shown with a style very similar to that of Plautilla, see above) (**48.17**, **colour plate 19**). Marble portraits, however, more frequently show the style with the slightly higher, larger bun as worn by Julia Maesa and the wife of Balbinus on his sarcophagus (AD 238), although with hair tucked behind the ears. The hair could be either straight or waved, and the bun of one or two spiralled plaits; but either way the top of the plaits form two distinctive 'wings' under the ears when seen from the front (cf **47.16, 48.17**)

c.AD 240 – c.AD 268

Sabinia Tranquillina (wife of Gordian III: coins of AD 241-4) is shown with two hairstyles: the low bun, and a new style where the heavily waved hair is brought to the back of the neck, plaited or braided and then pinned up the back of the head, sometimes so high that the top is just visible on the top (**48.18-9**). Marble statues show that this was a wide, flat bun, the details of which are often only sketchily carved. Some statues seem to depict the bun as a wide multi-strand braid of hair, with contoured plaits but without any representation of individual lines of hair as depicted on the rest of the hair, while others show a lattice incised over the top of a featureless bun, as if depicting a net covering the hair. The same style was worn by a number of the wives of the succeeding short-lived Emperors. A different hairstyle, not shown on coins, which might belong to the same period, had the hair forming wings behind the ears, then being lightly twisted up the back of the head and onto the top, with the ends tucked back in. It is difficult to see how such a loose twist could ever be kept up (**48.20**).

c.AD 270 – c.AD 307

Ulpia Severina (wife of Aurelian) developed the style worn by preceding Imperial women by bringing the bun right down to the forehead, where the ends are tucked in (**48.21**). The section of bun over the forehead could be decorated with spherical headed hairpins or pearls sewn onto the net. A wall painting from a catacomb shows two pins or pearls (**35.2**), while a portrait from Egypt clearly shows three gold-headed pins.

c.AD 307 – c.AD 326

Helena (mother of Constantine) is shown wearing either a hairstyle similar to that of Ulpia Severina or another where an extremely thick plait was wrapped round her head in the manner of a diadem (**48.22**). On some statues the plait is decorated with jewels. Fausta

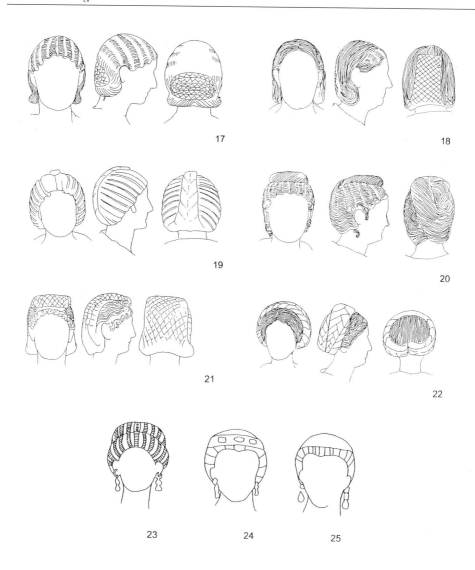

48 Hairstyles of the third to sixth centuries. 17 AD 218–40; 18–20 AD 240–68; 21 AD 307–26; 23 late fourth century 24–5 fifth century

(wife of Constantine I), however, is shown with two hairstyles that are closer to styles of two or three centuries earlier: waved hair brought back to a flat-topped bun wrapped round with a plait low on her neck as worn *c*.AD 14 - *c*.AD 37, or sections of hair twisted and brought back to a coiled plaited bun high on the head, similar to some styles worn by Faustina II and others *c*.AD 145 -160. These simple styles matched her husband's change from the Tetrarchic look to a neo-first century appearance, harping back to an earlier age. It was, however, a short-lived fashion.

c.AD 326 onwards

After this date, it is almost impossible to distinguish the hairstyles of Imperial women on coins as they are invariably depicted with elaborate diadems. As the Imperial family increasingly used diadems and elaborate head-dresses to distinguish themselves from ordinary people (**colour plate 2**), fashionable women could no longer copy the Empress' hairstyles in the same way as in previous centuries. The fact that respectable Christian women now had to keep their head covered inside as well as outside the house also meant that there was less opportunity for display of elaborate coiffures. St Paul wrote that as a woman was made from man and for man she should wear a veil on her head, a symbol of man's authority over her (1 *Corinth.* 11, 10). The hair was now fully covered so that not even a curl was visible, and the fashion for elaborate display was past. In the late fourth century, Serena, the wife of Stilicho has a bulky hairstyle looking rather like a cottage loaf, which is quite clearly covered in cloth (**48.23**).

Fifth century

In the fifth century the ladies of the court of Theodora (AD 527-65) also had their hair concealed beneath hoods. There are two main styles, the first of which had a cap that framed the face closely, with a narrow horizontal band that could be either plain or decorated (**48.24**). On some women this band gave the cap a cottage-loaf profile, similar to Serena's hairstyle. The second style consisted of a tight-fitting cap covered by a larger hood in a different colour (**48.25; colour plate 2**).

Hair pins

The elaborate hairstyles were kept in place by straight pins made of bone or metal, but as already noted, these are not represented on statues. The Egyptian mummy portraits sometimes show the pins, including some long pins stuck through hair piled up on top of the head in a way that is more ornamental than functional (**colour plate 14**). There are also a couple of burials where hair with hairpins still in place have survived. A mummified head of a 15-year-old girl dating to the early second century (now in the Petrie Museum, London) shows a plait drawn up to the top of the head and held in place by four pins (two of bone, one of tortoiseshell and one of silver). Another head, from York, shows a loose bun of hair held in place by two remaining jet pins. The second-century burials at Les Martres-de-Veyre, France include the remains of two simple plaits, while a fourth-century grave at Poundbury has the remains of five- and six-strand braids.

Hair oil

Women, like men, used hair oil. In the first century, Martial wrote a gift tag for a gold hairpin which suggests the use of hair oil: 'so that your moistened hair may not damage your bright silks, insert a pin to hold up your twisted hair' (*Ep.* 14.24), while in the second century, the narrator of *The Golden Ass*, in describing his obsession with women's hair, talks of hair 'anointed with the lotions of Arabia' and mentions worshippers of Isis with oil-moistened hair (Apuleius 2.9; 11.10). The plait of hair from Poundbury, and hair from another woman in the same cemetery, seem to have been oiled. The waves in the hair frequently seen on the portraits may have been made using oil and finger-styling or heated

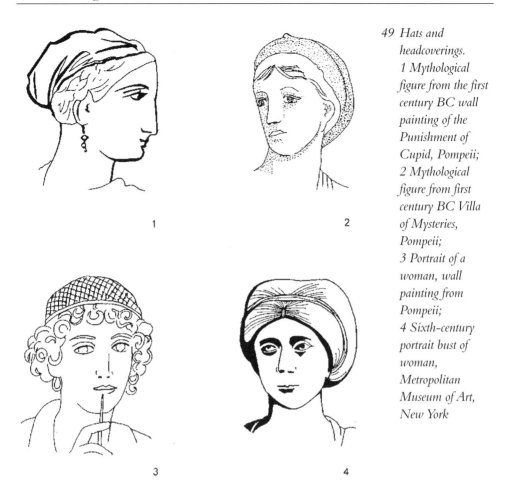

49 Hats and headcoverings. 1 Mythological figure from the first century BC wall painting of the Punishment of Cupid, Pompeii; 2 Mythological figure from first century BC Villa of Mysteries, Pompeii; 3 Portrait of a woman, wall painting from Pompeii; 4 Sixth-century portrait bust of woman, Metropolitan Museum of Art, New York

curling irons. Statues can show the same hairstyle with both waved or smooth hair, so it would seem this was a personal choice.

Hairnets

Hairnets made out of gold were sometimes worn by the rich during the first century AD, although as hairstyles grew more complicated, hairnets went out of fashion (**49.3**). According to a biographer of Severus Alexander, hairnets were also known in the early third century, when the Emperor includes one in a list: 'the women of the imperial household should be content with one hairnet, a pair of earrings, a necklace of pearls, a diadem to wear while sacrificing, a single mantle ornamented with gold, and one robe with a decorated border, not to contain more than six ounces of gold' (SHA, *Severus Alexander*, 41.1). However, as the *Scriptores Historia Augustae* was written in the late third or fourth century, when hairnets worn over the wide plait may have come back into use, this may be an anachronism. The late fourth-century grave portrait of Aelia Arisuth shows her dressed in a blue tunic with a short white mantle wrapped round her shoulders and her hair covered by a large white cap. In the fifth century, the whole of the head was covered by a snood, sometimes gathered at the front (**49.4**). Some seem to have been made out of cloth, but surviving examples from Egypt are made out of sprang-work.

Hats

Modest women were supposed to keep their heads covered when out of doors, but this generally took the form of draping their mantle over their head rather than wearing a hat since the elaborate hairstyles frequently made hats impossible (**41**). In the first centuries BC and AD, there are some references to the turban (*mitra*) being worn by rich women, and it is possible this is the cloth wrapped round the head like a headscarf seen on women in Hellenistic paintings (**49.1-2**). The freedman's cap could also be worn by women on occasion; women who had probably been freed in the will of the deceased are shown wearing it on the reliefs of the Tomb of the Haterii in Rome (**50**). Straw hats like those worn by men would have been worn by labourers or travellers, but they were never fashionable for the rich. In towns, wealthy women would have been protected from the harmful rays of the sun – tans were definitely unfashionable – by parasols.

Parasols

Parasols (*umbellae* and *umbracula*) were used to protect rich women from the sun. Martial wrote a gift tag for one: 'accept a parasol to defeat the fierce sun' (*Ep.* 14.28) while in *The Golden Ass* a Triton 'protects Venus from sunburn with a silk parasol' (4.31). Although women could carry one themselves, they could equally get a slave or better yet an admirer to carry it for them, as Ovid suggests: 'do you yourself hold her parasol outstretched upon its rods' (*Art of Love* 2.209). A relief from a tombstone from Rome shows that the parasols could be folded in the manner of the modern umbrella (**51.1**). A wall painting of a female figure, perhaps the personification of summer, has one decorated with tassels (**51.2**), while Juvenal refers to a parasol of green (*Sat.* 9.50).

50 Freedwoman with loose hair and wearing a cap at the funeral of her ex-mistress, Tomb of the Haterii, Vatican Museum

51 Parasols and fans. 1 Folded parasol, bas relief from Avezzano, Italy; 2 Allegorical figure holding parasol, wall painting from Pompeii, Musée du Louvre; 3 Ivory fan handle (one of a pair) from grave in York; 4 Allegorical figure of 'summer', mosaic from Djebel Oust, Tunisia; 5 Woven palm fan from Egypt, Staatliche Museen zu Berlin; 6 The mistress from the Lord Julius mosaic, Carthage

Fans

Women used fans (*flabella*) to keep themselves cool. Some were folding, with handles made of ivory such as those found at York (**51.3**), perhaps with the skin made from strips of vellum sewn together as on early medieval examples. A tombstone from Carlisle and a mosaic from North Africa both show this form of fan (**51.4;** see also **71**). Others were rectangles of woven palm set on a long handle (**51.5**), while there is literary evidence for fans made from peacock feathers (Claudian, *Eutropius* 1.109; Propertius, *Elegies* 24.11). Martial refers to leek-green and purple fans (*Ep.* 3.82.11; 10.30.15). Men did not usually carry fans, but they could still be fanned by slaves.

FOOTWEAR

Sandals

During those periods when it was fashionable to wear tunics that reached the floor, it is not always possible to see what women wore on their feet. In the first and second centuries women are shown wearing sandals with delicate thongs from between the big toe and its neighbour, to half-way down the sole. On portrait statues the thongs are sometimes only painted onto the stone, but when depicted, the thongs were often cut into arrow-shapes (**52**). This central section could also be decorated with pearls (**colour plate 15**; Pliny, *Nat. Hist.* 9.6.114). Very often there was another thong round the back of the foot (**53**; see also the seated woman – probably a mythological figure – in **colour plate 13**).

    In mainstream art women are shown wearing these sandals with bare feet, but slotted socks could also be worn with them (**20**; **colour plate 15**). Although these sandals had delicate uppers, they usually had thick soles, often several centimetres thick on sculptures. Thick soles would make sandals more robust and more suitable for wet roads and bad weather. Pliny mentions cork being used for the soles of women's winter shoes (*Nat. Hist.* 16.13.34), and sandals with raised soles of cork or scraps of leather have been found in the archaeological record. Thick soles could also be used to give height to short women; Juvenal refers to a woman wearing a raised Greek boot favoured by actors to make her taller (*Sat.* 6.506). The lower classes probably wore a more enclosed shoe or boot, but their footwear is often only depicted very sketchily.

Shoe-sock

Whether soft shoes or true socks, *socci* were also worn by women. Both Caligula and Nero were criticised by later biographers for wearing womanish *socci*, but it is not clear whether the shoe-socks themselves or their decoration were considered effeminate.

Boots

The fourth-century short tunics made footwear very much more visible, and women are almost invariably shown wearing ankle boots. Some seem to have a row of dots up the front (see the female figure to the left, **colour plate 8**), which may possibly be decoration such as pearls. Diocletian's Edict, however, refers not only to women's boots, but to

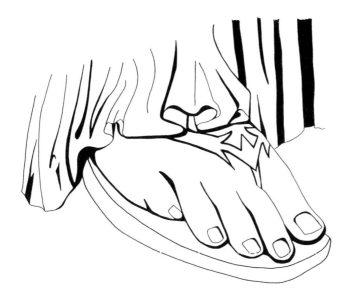

52 Sandal, early second-century statue, British Museum

double- and single-soled oxhide shoes as well as to *socci,* so there was clearly some choice of footwear. In later periods, it is assumed that enclosed shoes or boots were still being worn, but they are almost always concealed by ground-length tunics. One of the few exceptions is the figure of Rebecca in the *Vienna Genesis* manuscript, who shows one ankle and is clearly wearing orange-red boots.

Clogs

Women also wore wooden-soled clogs (see p63). The narrator in the *Satyricon* was attacked by a 'half-blind old woman wrapped round in the dirtiest of linen and set up on unequal wooden soled sandals' (Petronius, 95). The example from Les Martres-de-Veyre, France seems to have been lined with sheepskin, although none of the straps has survived (**54**).

Colour

As well as being decorated with pearls, shoes could be decorated with punched designs, openwork, or even gold leaf. Ovid writes of 'snow-white shoes' (*Art of Love* 3.271), while a bandit disguised as a woman also wore 'thin white shoes' (Apuleius, *Ass* 7.8), and Fortunata wore Greek-style white shoes decorated with gold (Petronius 67.4). Tertullian writes indignantly of a brothel-overseer wearing mullet-red shoes (*Mantle* 4.10), which might suggest that this colour was as symbolic of rank for women as it was for men. A third- or fourth-century shoe from London has an inner layer of leather in a contrasting pale colour to the outer purple layer, which is cut into a delicate openwork pattern, and sewn with gold thread. Theodora wears white and gold shoes decorated with blue to match her tunic, while the ladies of her court wear orange-red shoes (**colour plate 2**). This orange-red seemed to be a popular colour in the sixth century, for it is also used for the footwear of the Virgins in procession and almost all of the women in the biblical scenes in the mosaics of Basilica of St Apollinare Nuovo, as well as many women in the

53 Sandals, bas relief from Avezzano, Italy

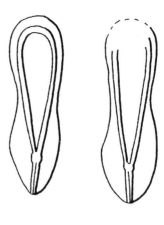

54 Wooden clogs from second-century tomb at Les
    Martres-de-Veyre, France

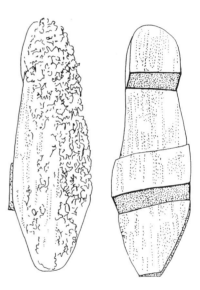

Vienna Genesis and the *Rossano Gospels*. The few women not wearing orange-red shoes have black or brown boots or shoes instead.

SPECIAL COSTUMES

Wedding dress

Roman marriage did not require a set ceremony as nowadays, as it was more a matter of mutual agreement, public acknowledgement and the fact that the couple lived together in the husband's house. As documentary evidence of a marriage was often needed for legal reasons when dealing with property, marriage contracts might be drawn up, but they were not compulsory and their presence or absence had no bearing on the validity of the marriage. A celebration in front of witnesses helped to provide the public acknowledgement and proof of mutual agreement, so weddings could be celebrated in style, including torch-lit processions, feasts and a specially decorated bridal chamber, by those with money.

Except for the wealthiest Romans, the concept of special, elaborate clothing to be worn only on the wedding day is modern. In the past, it was more usual for a dress bought or made for the occasion to be worn afterwards. When the writer Laura Ingalls Wilder got married in 1885 she simply wore a dress that she had already started making as it would be brand new for the ceremony; it happened to be black, but its newness was more important than the colour.

There was, however, a recognised costume for Roman women rich enough to be able to afford it. The most important feature was the flame-coloured mantle (*flammeum*). Pliny uses the word *luteum* to describe the colour, the same word he uses to describe an egg yolk, so it was presumably dark yellow to orange in colour. The mantle was worn in the same way as the *palla*, but instead of the edge resting on the top of the woman's head, it was pulled forward to hide half of her face (**55.1**). This flame-coloured mantle was originally worn on an everyday basis by the Flaminica Dialis, the wife of the priest of Jupiter, and as she was unable to divorce, the mantle may have come to represent constancy and was therefore used in wedding celebrations.

A wreath of flowers and herbs was worn under the mantle, and the hair was dressed in a special manner using woollen ribbons of cloth (*vittae*). A single reference suggests that the hair was divided into six separate parts and there has been much discussion on what form this took, but the description relies solely on the interpretation of a single word, which has also been interpreted to mean 'twisted and bound' or 'cut'. As the hairstyle is usually concealed under the mantle and wreath, the most that can be said about it is that it was bulky (**55.1**).

The other, less important elements of the costume included a straight tunic (*tunica recta*) that was traditionally specially woven for the occasion. One author says it was worn the night before the wedding, along with a flame-coloured hairnet. For most women this 'straight' tunic was probably no different from a normal tunic, and it was certainly fastened under the bust in the usual manner, with a woollen cord tied in a Herculean (reef) knot that only the bride's new husband could untie. The poet Catullus also mentions flame-coloured *socci* (61.8-10). This outfit was worn by brides in the first century, and Claudian is still referring to a flame-coloured mantle worn by Serena when she married Stilicho in the late fourth century (*Stilicho* 1.80-4).

Nightwear

Wearing special clothes for bed (as nowadays) does not appear to have been universal. Many people would either have worn their day-wear, or nothing at all. Some modest women apparently did wear clothes, such as the wife Martial describes, who wore 'breastband, tunic and obscuring mantle' (*Ep.* 11.104) while Propertius talks of a woman sleeping wrapped in a mantle and another wearing a night-cap of silk (*Elegies* 3.21.8; 2.29.15). There is some evidence that a night gown might have become more popular in the later period, when the word *camisia* is used for it.

55 Bridal and religious costumes. 1 Bride, bas relief from sarcophagus, Mantua, Italy; 2 Vestal Virgin, third-century statue, Museo Nazionale, Rome; 3 Priestess of Isis, relief from tombstone, Athens; 4 Priestess of Isis, relief from tombstone, Athens

Religious costumes

Roman priestesses sometimes wore a distinctive form of costume to distinguish them from other women. Tertullian refers to women choosing their religion purely for the sake of the clothes:

> some are initiated into [the mysteries] of Ceres for the sake of an all-white dress or the honour of ribbons (*vittae*) and the privilege of a [religious] cap, while those with a contrary disposition towards dark clothes and a dull woollen covering for the head run free on Bellona's mount; others commend Saturn for the ostentatious purple stripes and the red Galatian wrap. (*Mantle* 4.10)

The clothes of the religious cults were often old-fashioned, or used unusual methods of fastening and were usually closer in style to that worn by goddesses than their fellow humans. It is noticeable how much use was made of brooches to fasten shawls or mantles, at a time when brooches were usually reserved for male costume in mainstream fashion (**55.2, 4**). This may either be the influence of provincial clothing being brought in with the often foreign cults, or of the goddesses, whose tunics were fastened with brooches in the old-fashioned manner.

Vestal Virgins

The Vestal Virgins are the most well-known of Roman priestesses, holding a very special role in Roman public life. Images of Vestal Virgins show a variety of tunics and hairstyles, and there is some debate about whether they actually represent what the women themselves wore. Generally, their dresses seem to be based on Hellenistic tunics, with long overfolds. The most important elements, as with the bride, was the covering for the head. Their hair was concealed with the *infula*, red and white woollen ribbons coiled round the head and tied at the back, with the ends hanging down over the shoulders in long loops (Servius 10.538). These ribbons are shown either arranged almost as a turban, or in the form of a simple headband. Over this they usually wore a short white mantle with a purple border, fastened by a brooch (*suffibulum*) (**55.2**), although some images show them bare-headed, or simply wearing a mantle.

Priestesses of Isis

The costume that seems to have been worn by these priestesses was also based on ancient clothing; in this case, that of the goddess herself. The costume consisted of a fringed mantle fastened with a knot, worn over a ground-length tunic with long, tight-fitting sleeves. The mantle was a long rectangle of cloth, fringed on the short sides; the mid-point on the long side was held in a bunch between the breasts with the two ends taken under the arm and over the opposing shoulders. The two ends were then tied in a knot with the cloth held between the breasts, with the fringed ends hanging down below. Statues of the goddess from the third century BC show her wearing a very similar outfit, although in this case the mantle is the main item of dress and it is shown as thin and figure-hugging, unlike the rather more robust Roman interpretations of it.

This is shown on some tombstones of priestesses, but it is not clear whether the outfit was worn only for religious activities or for everyday use (**55.3**). There is even the possibility that the priestesses were depicted *as* Isis and never actually wore the costume in real life.

Other priestesses

A tombstone of a priestess of Isis shows the woman not wearing her mantle tied in an Isis knot but folded over and fastened on her right shoulder (**55.4**). Another tombstone of a priestess of Jupiter from Mainz shows another woman wearing her mantle fastened in a similar way. A statue, now in the Vatican Museum, of a young girl holding a sacrificial dish in one hand, has her mantle folded to form a long narrow band over her shoulder and across her body, which is held in place by her belt. All these unusual ways of wearing the mantle would distinguish a priestess from normal women.

Mourning

Women in mourning wore dull-coloured clothes (see p27). The essence of mourning was to demonstrate grief by a lack of interest in personal appearance, so women are often also shown with their hair long and loose (**49**). There seems to have been no costume particular to the widow.

JEWELLERY

Women completed their costume with jewellery, the most common items of which were necklaces, earrings, finger-rings and bracelets. These could be made from a number of materials – gold, silver, copper alloy, iron, glass, bone, jet, amber and precious or semi-precious stones – depending on the wealth of the woman. Gold was the preferred metal for those who could afford it, probably because of its warm colour; although some jewellery is known in silver (particularly finger-rings) it seems to have been preferred for domestic plate. Roman jewellery on the whole depended on colour rather than glitter for effect, so the most sought after and expensive jewellery was made from pearls rather than diamonds. The Romans knew of diamonds, but they had no way to cut them and generally they were used as drills or engravers rather than jewellery. Modern gem stones have faceted faces and are set in foil to let the light catch them and make them glitter, but although the Romans used precious stones they usually left them in their natural state. Emeralds were particularly popular as they form hexagonal crystals and only need to be drilled to be used as beads. The most popular shape of stones, according to Pliny, were those with an elongated or lentular shape, while those with sharp angles were least regarded (*Nat. Hist.* 37.75.196).

Jewellery was priced according to the weight of precious metal and the number of stones used while craftsmanship, however exquisite, rarely added to the value. A wedding contract of AD 260 from Egypt that lists the dowry of the bride describes the jewellery by weight:

> a necklace in common gold . . . . of the kind called *maniaces*, having a stone and weighing apart from the stone 13 quarters, a brooch [?] with five stones set in gold, weighing apart from the stones four quarters, a pair of earrings with 10 pearls weighing apart from the pearls three quarters, a small ring weighing a half quarter . . . . making the total of the whole dowry one mina and four and a half quarters of common gold and for the valuation of the clothing 620 *drachmae*. (OP 1273)

The fictional Trimalchio tried to impress guests by pointing out that his wife had golden jewellery (including armlets, anklets and a hairnet) weighing 6.5lbs (2.9kg), while he had an armlet of 10lbs (4.5kg). To prove his point, he then proceeded to weigh the jewellery in front of his guests (Petronius, *Satyricon* 67). Then, as now, the amount of jewellery worn would have depended on the occasion and on the taste of the woman involved. Pliny complained about Lollia Paulina, a consort of Nero, being overdressed for 'an ordinary betrothal banquet', being 'covered with emeralds and pearls interlaced alternately and shining all over her head, hair, ears, neck and fingers, the sum total amounting to the value of 40,000,000 *sesterces*' (*Nat. Hist.* 9.58.117).

Designs in precious metals were often copied in cheaper materials for the lower classes. The designs also changed over time, with a general trend towards more flamboyant and ornate designs. Gold coins – set in pendants, bracelets and finger-rings – and intricate openwork designs became ever more popular from the second century onwards.

Pearls

According to Pliny, 'the whole value [of pearls] lies in their brilliance, size, roundness, smoothness and weight, qualities of such rarity that no two pearls are found that are exactly alike' (*Nat. Hist.* 9.56.112). During the first century, authors frequently used pearls as a symbol of expensive jewellery, and wrote disapprovingly of their use. Pliny also noted that 'women spend more money on their ears in pearl earrings, than on any other part of their person' (*ibid*, 11.50.136). Worse of all, in his opinion, were those people, male or female, who were so decadent that they sewed pearls not only onto their shoes but onto their socks (*ibid*, 37.6.17, 9.56.114).

In the late second century Fronto talks about the 'celebrated string of pearls, which every-one talks of', belonging to a woman called Matidia, and noted the interest in what would become of them after her death. It is clear from art that pearls continue to be the favourite jewel through-out the Roman period. The third- or fourth-century gold and glass portrait from Brescia shows the daughter with pearl necklace and earrings (**colour plate 16**), while the sixth-century mosaic of the Empress Theodora shows her wearing a head-dress set with pearls, with long strings of pearls hanging down either side of her face, and more pearls on her necklace and brooch (**colour plate 2**).

Finger-rings

Women also wore intaglios set in finger-rings, and like men, would wear rings on the upper joints (**56**). In the late first century Pliny mentions plain iron rings sent to the

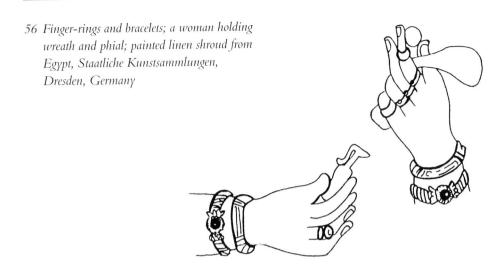

56 Finger-rings and bracelets; a woman holding wreath and phial; painted linen shroud from Egypt, Staatliche Kunstsammlungen, Dresden, Germany

woman as a betrothal ring, but this was not universal and there was no real concept of our modern engagement ring, nor were wedding rings obligatory (*Nat. Hist.* 33.4.12).

Bracelets

Simple bracelets made from copper alloy wire are extremely common finds in the archaeological record, and were made in a variety of styles. More elaborate, larger forms of bracelets were made in gold, and could be decorated with jewelled settings (**56**). Bracelets made up of glass or jet beads are also known.

Earrings

Earrings were worn in pierced ears. The simplest forms were loops, sometimes hung with a bead, that were often meant to be worn semi-permanently. Those who could afford a choice of earrings wore pendant earrings, which were made in a number of designs. A loop threaded with beads or pearls, a gem set in gold with a pendant pearl or bead below or a horizontal bar with three pendant pearls were all very common second- and third-century designs (**colour plates 14, 16, 20**). Pearls, as usual, were a popular stone, with drop-shaped ones particularly favoured (Pliny, *Nat. Hist.* 9.56.114). The future Emperor Vitellius, when sent from Rome to Lower Germany, 'took a valuable pearl from his mother's ear and pawned it, to defray the expenses of his journey' (Suetonius, *Vitellius* 7).

Necklaces

Few necklaces are shown in mainstream art other than a short string of large beads, frequently pearls. The Egyptian portraits often show three or four necklaces worn at the same time, from tight chokers to long loops over the breast, but it is unclear how common this was elsewhere in the Empire (**colour plate 14**). Due to the relatively high necklines of tunics, the short necklaces were often half-hidden (see the mother in **colour plate 16**); and there was definitely no plunging neckline to show off an elaborate necklace as was the fashion in later centuries.

57 *Necklace of gold with pearls and semi-precious stones. Early seventh-century, Staatliche Museen*
Preussischer Kulturbesitz, Berlin

The most common form of necklace was a string of small coloured beads, or a delicate
necklace of beads threaded onto twists of gold wire. The beads on the wire necklaces could
be all glass or precious stones in their natural state, in either case often alternating with
pearls. More elaborate forms had the beads joined by decorative elements such as
quatrefoils or Hercules knots (**colour plate 20**). More expensive necklaces had large
precious or semi-precious stones (or even paste) in gold settings, such as the necklace with
amethyst and emeralds now in the British Museum (**colour plate 20**).

In the fourth century, a fashion for large collar necklaces that covered the neck and half
the shoulders came in (**57, 42, colour plate 2**). The necklace from Egypt is made up of
separate plaques with a mixture of intricate openwork designs, and was originally set with
112 gems. The central settings are missing, but it still has pearls, emeralds and
aquamarines set in it (**57**).

Other forms

Other less common forms of jewellery included hair ornaments that hung down the central
parting, armlets worn on the upper arm, anklets, and body chains. These consisted of long
chains that crossed the body diagonally from shoulder to hip, with a large jewelled setting
where the chains crossed. The woman preparing for a bath depicted on a silver bucket in
Naples Museum wore one under her tunic, and continued to wear it while she bathed.

5 Children's clothing

Babies

Babies were routinely wrapped in swaddling clothes to keep them immobile. The swaddling clothes could take the form of either a blanket or cloth tied round the baby with bands or strips of cloth, or of a long strip of cloth wrapped round and round (**58**). The birth of the future emperor Clodius Albinus as described in the *Scriptores Historiae Augustae* provides some insight into the swaddling clothes of a new born baby. His father, Ceionius Postumus, wrote a letter announcing the birth: 'A son was born to me on the seventh day before the Calends of December, and so white was his body at birth that it was whiter than the linen cloth in which we wrapped him', a circumstance which lead to the name of the child, Albinus ('white'). Later, he was wrapped in bandages of a reddish colour, as was the tradition of his family (see p93 for full text).

The physician Soranus gave detailed instructions on the bandages to be used:

> take soft woollen bandages which are clean and not too worn out, some of them three fingers in breadth, others four fingers. Woollen, because of the smoothness of the material and because linen ones shrink from the sweat; soft, so as not to cause bruises when covering the body which is still delicate; clean, so that they may be light and not heavy, nor of evil smell, nor irritate the surface by containing natron; and not worn out, for whereas new ones are heavy,

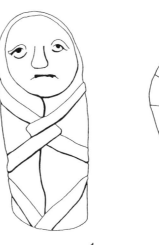

58 Babies in swaddling clothes.
1 Votive object, Musée Archéologique de Dijon, France; 2 Tombstone of Aeliola, Musée de Metz, France

1

2

59 Children depicted on the Ara Pacis, Rome

worn-out ones are too cold, and sometimes rough as well and very easily torn. They must have neither hems nor selvages, otherwise they cut or compress. (*Gynecology* 2.14[83])

He also gave detailed instructions on how to wrap the baby up, and recommended that the baby stay swaddled for between 40 and 60 days.

Children

There was not a great distinction between child and adult in the Roman world, as offspring, even as adults, were under the authority of their father until his death. In the poorer classes children could be less than 10 years old when they joined the adult world of work and helped their families earn a living. The minimum legal ages for marriage was 12 for a girl and 14 for a boy, although in practise it was generally a few years later. There was usually a ten-year age gap between husband and wife, so in aristocratic families women married for the first time in their early teens and men in their early twenties, while for the lower classes women tended to marry in their late teens and men in their late twenties.

In general, children wore the same clothes as their parents (**59**; see also father and son in **8** and **39**), – tunics, mantles and capes, in all their variations, as well as the toga for special occasions. There is, however, some evidence that young women sometimes wore a different form of tunic to that of their elders. Although some girls are shown in tunics belted under the bust, a Republican tombstone with a girl beside her mother shows the girl wearing a tunic belted at the waist, and a statue of a young girl standing beside a seated woman (presumably her mother) now at Chatsworth shows her in a tube-dress with a thigh length overfold, belted at the waist and worn over a sleeveless tunic. This undertunic may well be the linen garment called a *supparum* that Festus suggests was usually only worn by girls (M311). A sarcophagus now in the Louvre showing girls playing also shows the same type of dress (**60**). The advantage of this style is that by reducing the length of the overfold the tunic can be made longer for the growing girl.

On formal occasions children were made to wear the same costume as their parents, including even the toga. A tombstone from Ostia shows a five-year-old boy in the toga, while the procession of the Imperial family on the Ara Pacis shows boys of about two and six, although the chances of getting a child of two to wear a toga and keep it in order does seem rather remote. Boys wore the *toga praetexta*, a toga edged with a purple border, which was a form of toga also worn by magistrates.

60 Young girls playing a ball game, bas relief from sarcophagus, Musée du Louvre

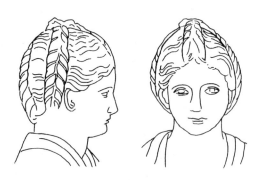

*61 Hairstyle of young girl, statue of
c.50 BC, Palazzo dei
Conservatori, Rome*

For girls there was no rite of passage between childhood and adulthood beyond marriage itself. Boys' coming-of-age as an adult citizen was marked by a ceremony when the *toga praetexta* was laid aside in honour of the all-white *toga virilis*. There was no fixed age for this ceremony, which was decided by the family, but it was generally around the age of 15 or 16. This ceremony would have been held only for the children of rich families, and it is not clear how long it continued after the first century. For men there was a period of 'adolescence' in their late teens and early twenties, between boyhood and marriage, which was often, in tradition at least, a time for profligate behaviour. There was no equivalent period for women, who moved straight from daughter to wife.

Hairstyles

It seems that as soon as a girl had hair long enough to pin up, it was worn up. Even relatively young girls, with hair only just below shoulder length, are shown with three plaits that are fastened together on the top of the head (**61**). The girl on the Ara Pacis is about 10 or 11 years old years and already has her hair tied in a bun like the older women (**59**).

6 Beauty

Women

At different periods, different parts of the female body have been seen as attractive – a neat ankle, a snow-white bosom, or a rounded shoulder – while the desired shape for the body has always changed over time, with various features of the body being either exaggerated or concealed. For example, in the late fifteenth century, women's dresses had a high waist-line and women are usually shown standing with an arched back and folds of their skirts held in front of their stomach to give an impression of pregnancy. In the nineteenth century, however, huge bell-shaped skirts emphasised a very narrow waist, while in the 1920s, fashionable women were expected to be flat-chested in their straight, low-waisted dresses.

Apart from the brief period for unbelted tunics in mainstream fashion during the fourth century, the rich Roman woman always had a high waistline under the bust, skirts long enough to cover the ankles, elbow-length sleeves and a relatively high neckline. The costume of the respectable woman could be very enveloping, as Horace pointed out when he compared the dress of a matron and a prostitute:

> In a matron, one can only see her face, for . . . . her long tunic conceals all else. But if you seek forbidden charms that are invested with a rampart . . . . many obstacles will then be in your way – attendants, the sedan, hairdressers, parasites, the *stola* dropping to the ankles, the mantle wrapped round – a thousand things which hinder you from a clear view. In the other – no obstacle. In her Coan silk you may see her, almost as if naked, so that she may not have a poor leg, an unsightly foot; you may measure her whole form with your eye. (*Sat.* 1.2.95-104)

The way for a respectable woman to show off her charms was to adopt the clothing of the brazen. Women could wear tunics of extremely thin cloth, so that although fully clothed, the shape of their bodies was visible, and there are numerous complaints about this fashion in literature. The best material to use was silk, which, since it had to be imported from China, was seen by some as yet another example of eastern fashions corrupting the weak. Pliny complained about the huge distances involved and the amount of work in preparing the thread 'to enable the Roman matron to flaunt transparent clothing in public' (*Nat. Hist.* 6.20.54) and Seneca of the 'clothes that hide nothing of the matron's body' (*Debates* 2.5.7).

Ovid's books *Painting the face* and *The Art of Love* are full of advice on how women could make themselves more attractive to men. In essence, he suggests that women should choose clothes and hairstyles to suit their colouring and body shape, and to emphasise their best features, whatever they were. In his companion book, *The Remedies of Love*, on how to fall out of love, he rather cynically comments that men 'are won by dress; all is concealed by gems and gold; a woman is the least part of herself' (343-4).

In the late Empire, as has been said, women's mantles generally became smaller and less concealing, but in contrast, their tunics covered more of the body. Necklines were hidden under collar necklaces, sleeves covered the arms to the wrists, and even the hair was concealed under snoods or caps. More than ever, women had to use their clothes and their jewellery, rather than the appeal of naked flash, to make themselves attractive.

Men

The desired shape for a man's body has also changed over time, from the unbelted calf-length tunics of the thirteenth century, to the skin-tight hose and codpiece of the sixteenth century and the tucked in waists and padded shoulders of the early nineteenth century. The Roman tunic covered some or all of the arms, and was generally belted at the waist or hips, leaving most of the leg bare; even when trousers were adopted, they were skin tight hose so that the shape of the legs were still visible. The exact length of the tunic varied depending on who wore it, with soldiers wearing short tunics and senators long ones, although there was obviously some room for personal choice. Horace writes of 'Maltinus who walks with his garments trailing low; another, a man of fashion, wears them tucked up indecently high as far as his waist' (*Sat.* 1.2.25-30). Men who took too much care over their appearance were regarded as either popinjays or effeminate, but there was also the usual tension between conservative older men and fashionable youths over what was acceptable. As there was little scope for variety in the cut of the tunic or mantle, fashionable young men had to use bright colours to make themselves attractive, and Quintilian pointed out that 'purple and scarlet clothes go ill with grey hairs' (*Instit,* 11.1.31). Men were supposed to be tall and athletic, and are usually shown with a darker skin tone than women, consistent with a healthy outside life. Some men, like the women, needed help with their looks, and wore shoes with raised soles to make them taller, or resorted to wigs, curled their hair with tongs, plucked out all their body hair or even wore beauty patches.

7 Provincial clothing

INTRODUCTION

The provinces of the Roman Empire stretched from Spain to Syria, from Scotland to Egypt, and covered a great many different nations and tribes. The Romans imposed their rule on these people, set up an administration system and demanded taxes, but they also accepted that different people had different cultures and did not attempt to convert them all to an Italian Roman way of life.

Outside the Mediterranean region, the people in the provinces could be divided into three broad groups. The smallest group were the administrators and civilian and military leaders who were outsiders – usually from the Mediterranean region – such as the Provincial Governor and his staff, and the Commanding Officers of legions and auxiliary units. The second group were people native to the area but who adopted a Roman way of life, such as the rich ruling classes and those who lived in towns and followed a money-based economy. Lastly there was the third group, mainly the rural dwellers, who were very little influenced by the Roman way of life and continued to live their lives as they always had.

Mainstream Roman costume would have been seen in the provinces on the statues and busts of the Imperial family that would be found in every major city or town. The outsiders, the Roman administrators, would also have worn their own costume, and even the toga would have made an appearance in the palaces of the governors on official occasions. It is likely that some of the members of the native ruling class adopted Italian fashions. Tacitus, for example, mentions Agricola introducing Roman clothing to the Britons amongst other examples of the trappings of the Roman way of life: 'the wearing of our dress became a distinction, and the toga was frequently worn' (*Agricola* 21.2), and this may have trickled down to other layers of society.

The second group of people also followed a Roman way of life. One element of this was the adoption of the Roman method of burial with a grave marker made out of stone with a Latin or Greek inscription and frequently also a portrait of the deceased. These people could afford a tombstone, sometimes quite elaborate, and had it made to a Roman pattern – and yet they are shown wearing local costume rather than mainstream Roman fashion.

Although there is little evidence for what the third group of people, those least touched by a Roman way of life, would have worn, it is likely that the pre-Roman fashions continued for both men and women in some areas. In Gaul and Britain, it is clear that in pre-Roman times trousers were the most important item of clothing, and while in Roman times they were generally abandoned in favour of a loose, unbelted tunic, in rural areas trousers may well have still been worn.

62 Tombstone showing both native and mainstream fashions. Second-century, Landesmuseum Joanneum, Graz

Provincial costume may have changed over the centuries, just as mainstream fashion did. The following sections, however, simply give an introduction to the most typical costume in the different areas of the Empire without following its history in any detail. Looking at provincial costume as a whole, there are two striking points to consider. First, it is often the women who retained their native fashions while the men adopted Greek or Roman fashions, so that a gravestone can show a woman in native costume and the man in a toga or in a Greek tunic and mantle (**62**). Secondly, women's costume also tended to be more distinctive, and it is particularly noticeable that both the brooch and the hat play a much larger role than in mainstream fashion.

The best evidence for provincial clothing comes from tombstone portraits showing the deceased in the manner they wished to be commemorated. Another source of evidence is the images of prisoners-of-war used by Romans to decorate triumphal monuments. The danger of these depictions of course is that they may be more stock images of barbarians than fully accurate portrayals, but many of them show quite detailed non-Roman clothing and at the very least give a general idea of what these people would have worn.

Mosaics of the late Empire show people of all ranks wearing the late form of tunic decorated with roundels. It is not clear if native fashions died out to be replaced by a more universal fashion, or whether these images owe more to mosaic pattern-books than to local fashions. It is clear, however, that some forms of native costume are not depicted beyond the second century.

The following sections are not meant to be a comprehensive province-by-province examination of costume, but instead are intended to give a flavour of the varied styles of dress worn in the different areas of the Empire.

Barbarians

Romans considered the wearing of skins and furs to be an attribute of 'barbarians' even if worn by their own auxiliary troops. Tacitus described how a disguised Germanicus wore

63 Greek costume. 1 Tombstone of couple, Athens; 2 Tombstone of Eutychia, Athens

a 'wild-beast's skin over his shoulders' when he moved incognito amongst his own troops, while the army under the Emperor Vitellius presented 'a savage sight, dressed as they were in shaggy skins of wild beasts' (*Annals* 2.13; *Histories* 2.88). Claudian dismissed Rufinus as being 'thorough in his barbarity [because he] draped tawny skins of beasts about his breast' (*Rufinus* 79). Fur had no significance as an indicator of wealth as happened in the medieval and later periods.

Greece
Men
The male Greek costume was adopted in a number of countries where there had been Greek rule or influence before the Romans, so that under the Empire it was almost as widespread as Italian fashion. As has been seen, it was even worn at Rome. The costume consisted of a calf-length tunic, often unbelted, with a large mantle worn over the top (called a *himation*, the equivalent of the *pallium*), and openwork shoes (**63.1**). Soldiers and hunters wore belted knee-length tunics with cloaks.

Women
Female Greek costume had also influenced Roman costume as can be seen by the adoption of the gap-sleeved tunic, the belt high under the bust, and the large, all-enveloping mantle. However, gravestones from Greece show that a different form of tunic

was fashionable during the Roman period. This was full length with elbow-length sleeves; sometimes they were belted under the bust, but more commonly at the waist (**63**). Daughters or female slaves wore a tube-dress with a long overfold, belted at the waist, possibly over a short-sleeved undertunic (**63.2**).

Syria

Like many provinces, the coastal cities of Syria were more Romanised than the cities in the interior. The large trade city of Palmyra, some way inland, has a large collection of tombstones and statues that show both Roman and native styles of dress.

Men

Tombstones or painted burial chambers show the men dressed in two different styles of costume: they either wore Greek costume consisting of tunic and mantle (see above), or tunic, mantle or cloak and trousers based on Iranian and Parthian fashions (**64.1**). The Parthian tunic was mid-thigh in length, sometimes with side splits, with long, tight-fitting sleeves. It was decorated round the neck, wrists and hem, and frequently had an extra central stripe down the front (sometimes replaced by two stripes in the third century). The tunic is always shown with plentiful, stylised folds, and although the clothes may well have been made of thin cloth, the excessive use of folds must be an artistic convention. The tunic had a thin belt, often decorated, fastened with a reefknot and with the two long ends tucked under the belt, leaving the very characteristic two loops on either side (**64.2**). The man in Figure **64.1** has a slightly more unusual belt, with a narrow cord for the actual tie. Serving boys, probably slaves, are shown wearing a baggy tunic with elbow-length sleeves. Underneath they wear an undertunic with a fringed edge, visible on one side only under the hem of the overtunic.

Over the tunic, the men either wore a large mantle in the Greek manner that was mid-calf in length and hid most of the tunic underneath, or they wore a much smaller cloak fastened on the right shoulder with a circular brooch. The brooch was pinned in such a way that the hole left for the neck was very large, and it would slip down the left arm (**64.1**). The cloak, unlike the mantle, often had a decorated border.

The trousers were baggy, Iranian in style, and are shown with as many fine folds as the tunic. The trousers narrowed at the ankle and were always worn tucked into ankle boots (if, indeed, they did not have integral feet like the hose), and usually had a central band of decoration down the front. Up until about AD 150, much of the trousers was hidden by loose over-trousers, similar to the idea of a cowboy's chaps; they were attached only at the sides of the leg, so that their top edge hung down at the front to show the trousers underneath (**64.2**). The top edge had another band of decoration.

A rarer item of dress, most common in the third century and shown worn by rich, important men, was the 'coat'. This was another item of Parthian dress, in some ways like a modern cardigan, open down the front and worn over another item of dress (in this case, the tunic), collarless and with tight-fitting sleeves (**64.3**). It could also be worn crossed over at the front and tied with a belt, in the manner of a modern dressing-gown.

Footwear consisted of highly decorated, soft ankle boots, either with a thin sole for indoor use, or a plainer version with a sole for either indoor or outdoor use. Hats are not

64 *Syrian costume. 1–2 Third-century tombstones of men from Palmyra; 3 Syrian god, bas relief from Rome; 4 Tombstone of unknown woman, Palmyra*

shown on the tombstones, apart from the tall cylindrical hat worn by the priests, sometimes decorated with a wreath half way up the hat. That late 'Roman' style decorated tunics were also worn can be seen by the fragment of tunic found in the city with the purple and white interlace roundel so frequently seen in late Roman art (**7.1**).

Paint surviving on the sculpture or tomb wall paintings gives some idea of the colour of the clothes; green trousers with a red stripe, pale red tunic with white central stripes worn under cloaks of white, pale green and light and dark brown. A man called Maqqai is shown wearing a red coat over a blue tunic with a red central band, and red trousers with a yellow stripe, while another image shows him in a blue coat. Boys are shown in red tunics and blue trousers. A man called Hairan, wearing a Greek-style tunic and mantle, is shown in white, presumably representing white linen. As all fragments of linen recovered from the city are undyed, the colourful clothes shown in art must have been made from wool or silk.

Women

Women wore an undertunic which could either have relatively narrow sleeves (sometimes with a decorated band half way between shoulder and elbow) or wide sleeves (sometimes fringed). Both versions had a band of decoration round the wrist, and two stripes down the front. Over the top they wore a tube-dress fastened on one shoulder only, the left, with a massive brooch. To begin with the brooches were trapezoidal in shape, but later huge circular ones, some the size of a fist, came into fashion. The brooch could have one or two keys hanging from it, or three pendant chains (**64.4**). Such large brooches would be very heavy, and would pull the overtunic down, suggesting that they must have also been pinned to the undertunic to keep them in position. The overtunic was worn belted at the hips, but as the tunic was bloused out over it, the form of the belt is uncertain. The women usually, although not always, kept their heads covered. They wore a decorated band with a turban over the top, both covered by a veil that reached to the hips or below.

Exquisitely carved busts of Palmyrene ladies covered in jewellery are justly famous, but such ostentation was not universal. Most women are shown only with earrings and bracelets, although they could have head- and central-parting ornaments, earrings, up to seven necklaces, the large brooch with pendant decoration and a number of bracelets and finger-rings. Sometimes wide anklets were also worn (**64.4**). The wife of Hairan, in a tomb dated AD 149/150, has an undertunic of green, with a red stripe, and an overtunic shown as white with folds picked out in brown, and black shoes. Another woman has a tunic of green with an off-white band edged in red.

Judaea

There are no contemporary portraits of Jews in the province during the Roman period, so an understanding of their costume has to come from a study of a few surviving garments and literary evidence. L. Roussin has made a study of this evidence, and the following depends heavily on her article in *The world of Roman costume*.

65 Judaean costume, as illustrated by a wall painting of the discovery of the baby Moses, Dura-Europos, Syria

Men

Men's costume was very similar to the basic Greek costume used extensively in the eastern Empire, consisting of a tunic and mantle. The usual set of a man's everyday clothing can be seen in the list giving the order in which clothes were removed at a bath: 'first he removes his shoes, then the hat, then the mantle, then he unfastens the girdle, then his tunic, and after he unties the undergarment' (*Tosefta Derech Evetz, Perek Ha Niknas 1*). Surviving examples of the tunic from a collection of *c.*AD 135 in the Cave of Letters show that it was made of two rectangles of cloth sewn together, decorated with two stripes. The mantle was rectangular and was distinguished from the mantles worn by other races by the fact that it had a tassel on each of the four corners (*Deuteronomy* 22:12), while examples from the Cave show that by the mid-second century mantles had the L-shaped corner decorations. Interestingly, Jews did not use hobnails in their shoes. This was a long-lasting tradition that had started during times of persecution, when the sound of hobnailed boots, or the imprint of hobnails in the ground, could instantly be recognised as those of Roman soldiers without danger of confusion. Men were supposed to wear only white, but although this remained common, it is clear that it was not always strictly enforced.

Women

The best evidence for women's costume comes from the wall-painting showing the finding of Moses from the synagogue of Dura-Europos in Syria, although this needs to be

131

treated with the usual caution. While the women with the Pharaoh's daughter wear Greek costume, the women of Moses' family and their attendants apparently wear native Jewish costume, similar in many ways to that worn in Syria. They have an ankle-length undertunic with wide, elbow-length sleeves and a shorter tube-dress over the top, fastened on the left breast. They have a hip-length veil over their heads, and their mantles (decorated with L-shapes) are wrapped round their hips with the top part folded over, although it is not clear how this is fastened (**65**).

The veil was an important part of the costume, as women by custom (but not by law) had to keep their head covered when outside. Italian Roman women were also supposed to keep their head covered when outside of course, but it seems that Jewish women were more strict on this point: 'among the Jews, it is so usual for their women to have the head veiled that this is the means by which they may be recognised' (Tertullian, *Crown* 4). Women were allowed to wear coloured clothes, excluding the colour red, which was regarded as the colour of non-Jewish women.

Egypt

Information on clothing in Egypt comes from two main sources; mummy portraits buried with the dead, and garments that have survived in Egypt's dry conditions. Mummy portraits executed on wooden panels and inserted into the wrapping of the mummy are most often only head and shoulder portraits, so the amount of information they can provide on clothing is therefore limited in some ways (**colour plate 14**). In the later period, half length or full length portraits were painted onto large pieces of linen that were then used as shrouds for the mummies (**colour plate 15**). Mummy portraits, of course, are only evidence for the costume of people who could afford the mummification process.

A huge number of cloth fragments have been recovered from Egypt, although only a small number of these are complete garments. The almost complete child's tunic now in the Laing Art Gallery, Newcastle (**colour plate 21**) has a tuck that shortens the tunic by some three inches (8cm). It is visible still sewn up on the inside of the tunic (the left hand side, near the accession number label) and unpicked on the incomplete side (to the right), with the once hidden cloth a brighter colour than the outer face of the tunic. A similar tuck is found on a surprising number of complete tunics from Egypt, and it is clear that instead of turning up the hem to shorten a tunic, the Romans preferred to put a tuck in at the waist.

Men

Men are almost always shown wearing white tunics, decorated with stripes of purple, red or dark brown, with a white mantle worn over one shoulder. Some men, identified as soldiers, wear a dark coloured cloak either fastened on the right shoulder with a brooch, or simply draped over the left shoulder in the manner of the mantle, but recognisable as a cloak because of the brooch left pinned to a fold. Later portraits seem to show an undertunic visible at the neckline, decorated in a very simple manner, which usually took the form of two sets of two lines, front and back. The later full-length portraits show men in mid-calf length tunics, wrapped up in a mantle almost as long, with simple sandals (**66.1**). Other late shrouds show men wearing tunics with purple and white roundels.

66 Egyptian costume.
1 Painted linen
shroud, Pushkin
Museum,
Moscow; 2 Sixth-
or seventh-
century painted
pot, Staatlichen
Museen zu Berlin

There are a number of portraits, both male and female, with a horizontal band of decoration in the area of the waist. Some clearly pass over both arms and must be related to burial rites rather than to costume, but there are some where the band is clearly on the body of the tunic, shown on a praying boy from a painted pot (**66.2**). A similar horizontal band was shown on the tunics of some mythological figures on decorated silver plate, and on the Christian figures from Lullingstone villa. In both of these examples, the band comes *above* a belt holding the tunic in, so it certainly seems to be a decorative element rather than a wide belt or sash, and it may be genuine fashion of the fourth century.

Women

There are no known depictions of the gap-sleeved tunic, although their existence in Egypt cannot be totally ruled out as the upper arms are not always shown, or are covered by the mantle. Where the full shoulder can be seen, the tunics have sewn sleeves, with stripes that run over the shoulder.

In the first and second centuries tunics were generally decorated with two stripes, often edged in gold in the paintings. There are no full-length portraits of this period, so the length of the tunic is unknown, and nor is it known if they were worn belted or unbelted. The mantle is shown draped round one or both shoulders (**colour plate 14**).

Sometime in the third century there was a change in fashion. An undertunic was worn, visible at the neck. Usually white in colour, whatever the colour of the overtunic, it was decorated with simple woven or embroidered patterns round the neckline. The body of a young girl found in a grave at Mostagedda wore three tunics, the innermost of which had braids of red wool woven in a lozenge pattern in white linen round neckline and sleeve, and a fringed hem, while the undertunic of the woman in **colour plate 13** had red decoration of infilled triangles at the neck, and a fringe at the hem. Such full-length shrouds show these tunics as being mid-calf in length and worn unbelted. In the larger portraits the mantle is shown carried over both arms so that it is draped down between them in a big loop. The mantle worn by the lady in **colour plate 13** is the same colour as the tunic, and therefore not very clear, but it seems to have been carried in the same way. These mantles could be decorated with the typical L- and H-shapes.

A couple of late third- or early fourth-century full-length portraits show women in calf-length tunics decorated with wide stripes, sometimes patterned. The shrouds are fragmentary, and have a large zone of decoration over the lower body, but in the waist zone they have an element of decoration that matches that of the tunic. If these are not part of a mantle, they may be a horizontal band of decoration as seen on the men's tunics (see above).

Two portraits of a similar date show women in white tunics with purple stripes. They have wrist-length sleeves to the undertunics which are tied at the wrist and at one or two other places up the arm, forming puffed sleeves (**42**). The neckline is hidden by the heavy collar-type necklaces of the fourth century. The mantles are decorated with roundels.

North Africa

The tombstones showing native influence are very basic in style, and therefore only very limited information can be gleaned from them. Pre-Roman reliefs from Carthage show men and women in long unbelted tunics, the women also with a long rectangular mantle worn pulled over the head. Roman period tombstones show folds in the clothes, depicted as parallel lines. Men seem to wear a tunic and mantle (**67.1**). At Ghirza, hunters and farmers are shown wearing very short, belted tunics. Women wore a ground- or ankle-length tunic with a long overfold, sometimes belted at the waist (**67.2**). On other figures the mantle, worn draped over the left shoulder and under the right arm, obscures the details of the tunic.

Spain

Spanish art outside mainstream art also relied on simple images of human figures for portraits (**68.1-2**). It is likely that details were added on in paint, so it is not clear if women wore their tunics unbelted or not. A gravestone of an innkeeper shows a servant probably wearing a short tunic belted either under the bust or at the waist, like other slaves and servants from elsewhere (**68.3**). However, there is an image on another tombstone of a person weaving who is shown with no folds above the area of the waist, and plentiful vertical folds below. The fact that the person could be wearing either a belted tunic with folds shown only below the belt, or a form of skirt or sarong, highlights the limitations of these forms of simple images. Strabo, in a section on the the Lusitania area, describes the costume of the natives: 'all the men dress in black, for the most part in coarse cloaks (*sagum*) in which they sleep . . . . but the women always go clad in long mantles and gay-coloured gowns' (*Geography* 3.3.7).

67 North African costume. 1 Tombstone of man, Carthage; 2 Tombstone of woman, Carthage

Gaul

J.P. Wild has carried out extensive research on the provincial clothing of the north-west provinces, including Gaul, Britain and Germany, and the following information for these particular areas is all based on his pioneering work. Both men and women wore a form of tunic Wild calls a 'Gallic coat', using the word in the sense of a medieval rather than a modern coat; in other words, it was a tunic to be worn inside and was not bad weather outerwear.

Men

The native dress of the southern Gauls originally included trousers; Pliny explains that the province of Narbonne was originally called Bracata because the inhabitants wore trousers (*braccae*), while Propertius describes a Belgic chief as wearing 'striped trousers' (4.10.43).

In the north, more Romanised Gauls wore the Gallic coat. The male version of it came to just below the knee, with wrist or elbow length loose sleeves, and a wide slit neckhole. It could have a relatively narrow body, with distinct sleeves (**69.2**), or it could be more caftan-like, with sleeves tapering to the wrist (**69.1**). The lower edge was frequently curved, and a few examples are fringed. It was always worn unbelted, even outside, and thus was very different to the mainstream tunic. It was usually worn over an undertunic, generally visible at the neck. A narrow scarf, usually tucked in at the neck, was also worn.

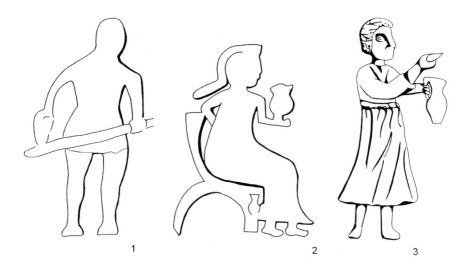

68 Spanish costume. 1 Man in short tunic, bas relief from tombstone, Museo Arqueológico, Burgos; 2 Tombstone of Aia, Museo Arqueológico, Burgos; 3 Serving woman, bas relief from tombstone, Museo Arqueológico de Mérida

The form of outer-wear worn with the gown was almost invariably the cape, either the long hooded version or the short shoulder cape. In the provinces, the long cape was not seen purely as poor weather or travelling clothes, but as a respectable covering, and men were quite happy to be shown wearing it on their tombstones (**72**). This outfit was worn by men such as doctors and wine-merchants as well as tenant farmers and slaves. The belted tunic was also worn, and is shown on men such as hunters, while mosaics show the later roundel-decorated tunics.

Women

Women wore the same form of gown, although naturally longer, and in their case the undertunic often more visible. The undertunic was generally ground length, with tight-fitting sleeves slightly longer than elbow length, and a rounded neck (**69.4, colour plate 18**). The gown worn over the tunic was approximately mid-calf in length, with wider, elbow-length sleeves, and could have a slit, rounded, or V-shaped neckline (**69.3-4**). As with the male version, it was not worn belted. Over the top was worn a mantle, generally smaller than the mainstream *palla*. It was often long and narrow and was worn like a modern long scarf, wrapped round the shoulders with a long end hanging down front and back (**69.3**). Other examples are even smaller, and were simply wrapped round the shoulders (**71**). Some women appear to wear a tight-fitting cape that covered all their hair.

Female slaves wore a short-sleeved tunic, usually ankle-length as befitted their lowly rank, tied with a belt closer in appearance to a sash than a cord, either at the waist or under the breast.

69 The Gallic coat. 1 Relief from tombstone, Trier, Germany; 2 School-boy, bas relief from Neumagen, Germany; 3 Tombstone from Regensburg, Germany; 4 Tombstone from Til-Châtel, France

A remarkable group of waterlogged graves from Les Martres-de-Veyre in France contained preserved clothes as well as other belongings and grave offerings. The six graves were discovered in 1851 and 1893 and were therefore not excavated in a scientific manner, and much information has been lost, but a number of clothes and shoes survived for study. In the grave of a woman, estimated to be about 30 years old, there were yellow, black and green beads and leather sandals with cork soles, while in the grave of another, older woman, there was a surviving plait of hair and wooden clogs (**54**). A pair of cloth ankle socks also came from this group of graves, but from which is unknown (**45.2**).

The most complete group came from the grave of a young woman and consists of a large tunic, a long length of cloth said by the excavator to be a belt, hobnailed shoes, knee-length socks and a plait of hair (**70**). The belt is extremely long, being 14ft (4.30m) including fringes, and may be an example of the sash-belt apparently worn by slaves in the north-west provinces, although why this woman was wearing one is not certain as it is clear from the gravegoods she was not a slave. The sash-belt may have been worn more commonly than the tombstone evidence would suggest, as part of an everyday working costume not usually commemorated by the deceased who preferred to be remembered shown in their 'Sunday best' clothes. The tunic has a large tuck round the waist, a feature seen on a number of tunics from Egypt (cf **colour plate 21**).

Britain

The Romanised version of native costume was basically the same as that worn in Gaul (see above).

Men

Not many tombstones of male civilians survive, but those that do suggest that the gown was also worn in Britain, as on the Carlisle tombstone of a mother and son, with the boy wearing an unbelted coat and undertunic under a cape, with the characteristic W-shaped lower edge (**71**).

Trousers, tunic and short cloak were probably the native dress of the Britons as of the Celtic and Germanic tribes. A fragment of a monumental statue from North Africa possibly shows a captive Briton, wearing a short cloak, no tunic, and trousers with different forms of checks on either leg. Martial refers to the baggy 'old trousers of a poor Briton' (*Ep.* 11.21.9).

Women

It is possible that in the first and second centuries women wore a form of tube-dress fastened with brooches; while there are no clear gravestone depictions of this fashion, pairs of brooches connected by a short chain are found in the archaeological record. From the late second century, if not earlier, women wore the Gallic coat (**71, colour plate 18**). Slaves are shown with the short sleeve tunic belted under the breast.

Rhine Valley

In this area, women wore a very distinctive costume while their husbands wore the usual Gallic outfit (**72**). The women's costume, however, had disappeared from gravestones by the late second century.

70 Romano-Gallic costume. The clothing and hair from Grave D at Les Martres-de-Veyre, France

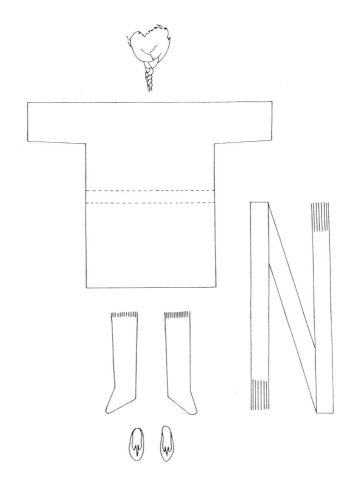

Women

The women wore a long undertunic with long, tight-fitting sleeves and a high neck, sometimes decorated with a frill. Usually a torc with a pendant was worn below the frill. Over the top of the undertunic was worn a tube-dress, fastened by brooches at both shoulders, although one side is sometimes shown as having slipped down the arm (**72**). Other examples have it fastened only on the right shoulder. Another central brooch pinned the overtunic to the undertunic, which was open down the front and fastened with a number of brooches set vertically.

Over the top of this the mantle was worn, draped under the left shoulder and fastened by a brooch on the right shoulder. This is an elegant but not very warm way of wearing a mantle, and it is not clear if another mantle was worn over the top for warmth, when needed, or if this mantle was unfastened and worn in a more conventional way; there are certainly depictions of the mantle being worn draped over one shoulder in the more conventional manner. Surviving paint on one tombstone shows a pale green undertunic, a red overtunic and a dark grey cloak.

71 Romano-British costume. Tombstone of mother and son, Tullie House Museum, Carlisle

72 Costume of the Rhine Valley. Tombstone of Blussus and Menimane, from Mainz, Germany

Some women wore a tight-fitting cap or hair net over their hair that was worn with a thick plait or pad of hair wrapped round the head above the brow. The tight-fitting cap shows both this ring of hair and sometimes also a small bun on the nap of the neck.

Lower Germany

In the area of the Ubian tribe women may have worn another distinctive form of clothing. The best examples of it are worn by mother goddesses, but sarcophagus portraits of mortal women shows them in the same form of costume, so it may be that the goddesses' costume does reflect the clothing of the area. Alternatively, it may be that the costume of the goddesses was worn by their priestesses, as with the priestesses of Isis (see p112).

The costume consisted of a ground-length undertunic and slightly shorter overtunic. The details of the upper part of the tunic are unknown, as over the top of this was worn a large semi-circular mantle worn shawl-like over both shoulders and fastened on the breast with a brooch. The most spectacular part of the outfit was the hat, a very large circular creation that looks almost halo-like from the front (**73**). Very few of them show any form of texture on them, so it is not very clear how they are made or fastened, but one example has a button with loops hanging down from it against one cheek, which is possibly a drawstring, while others have a decorated rod against their cheek that may be the end of a long decorative hair pin.

Germany beyond the Roman frontier
Men

Trousers were seen as the defining costume of both the Celt and the German. Tacitus describes the Germans as wearing:

73 Costume of Lower Germany. Statue of a Mother Goddess, Rheinisches Landesmuseum, Bonn, Germany

a thick cloak (*sagum*), fastened with a brooch . . . . They spend whole days on the hearth round the fire with no other covering. The richest men are distinguished by the wearing of underclothes; not loose, like those of the Parthians and Sarmatians, but drawn tight, throwing each limb into relief' (*Germania* 17).

A Roman relief of captured Germans shows them wearing a short cloak and nothing else, while a man from the tribe of the Suebi (with his hair worn in the characteristic knot) wears trousers and a short tunic over a bare chest. They were unlikely, however, to go bare-chested through a German winter, and other images show them in long-sleeved tunics.

The Germanic trousers had integral feet like the hose, as a surviving pair from a pool or bog deposit in Denmark shows (**74.2**). A tunic was found in the same deposits, with side slits and tight sleeves. The sleeves were made of woollen cloth woven to a different pattern to that of the body, and the faint patterning would have been visible (**74.1**).

Women

Tacitus describes German women as wearing: 'the same dress as the men, except that for the women a trailing linen garment, striped with purple, was frequently in use: the upper part of this costume does not widen into sleeves, and their arms and shoulders are therefore bare, as is the adjoining portion of the breast' (*ibid*, 17).

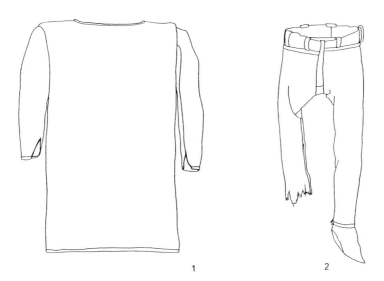

74 *Woollen clothing from a bog or pool deposit, Thorsborg, Denmark. 1 Tunic; 2 Trousers*

75 *Dacian costume from the Tropeaum Traiani, Bulgaria, c.AD 109. 1 Suebian prisoner with hair tied in knot; 2 Dacian prisoner; 3 Dacian woman*

76 Costume of Pannonia and Noricum; tombstone of a girl, Klagenfurt, Austria

Dacia and Moesia

Trajan's Column and the Adamklissi Trophy commemorating Trajan's victories in the Dacian Wars show both native male prisoners and their womenfolk. The fashions are very Germanic in style. The Dacians are shown in a tunic with wrist-length sleeves with high side slits, and a leather belt with a long hanging strap-end over ankle-length trousers (**75.2**). Dacian women wore a short-sleeved long tunic that from the direction of the folds suggests a drawstring at the neck (**75.3**). A mantle was worn tied round the waist or hips.

Noricum and Pannonia

Men

From Pannonia came the pill-box hat adopted by the Roman army in the late third century (Vegetius 1.20). Most men shown on tombstones are wearing togas or mantles (**62**).

Women

There are a number of surviving tombstones showing the typical first-century Norican costume for young women (shown bare-headed, and therefore possibly unmarried). It consisted of an ankle-length undertunic with a rounded neckline and skin-tight, wrist-length sleeves with wide cuffs (perhaps formed by decorative bands of tablet-weaving), worn under a tube-dress fastened on either shoulder with a large brooch with a tall upstanding tail. The upper tunic was shorter than the undertunic and on a tombstone from Klagenfurt it is shown tucked under, either pinned, or gathered by a drawstring

144

77 *Hats worn in Pannonia and Noricum. 1 Tombstone from Neumarkt, Austria; 2 Tombstone from Lendorf, Austria; 3 Tombstone of Umma, Landesmuseum, Vienna*

(**76**), although on other tombstones no such gathering is shown. The upper tunic was belted at the waist with a wide leather or cloth belt. From the belt hung two thin straps with decorated strap-ends and a central, wider strap with a plainer terminal. Some women also wore an extra brooch in the centre of the breast which seemed to have no functional purpose. The mantle, when used, was worn over both shoulders, in the manner of a shawl.

In the second century, the costume for married women had changed slightly. The undertunic had wider sleeves, and the upper tunic was belted under the bust and not at the waist (**62**). Most women also wore a hat with a curled or folded brim that sat on top of hair combed away from the face in two large rolls (**62, 77**). Other form of hats included a tall cylindrical hat swith a veil or mantle worn over the top and a large boat shaped hat, possibly made out of fur (**77.2-3**).

Conclusions

Modern everyday clothing is generally chosen for convenience and comfort and, apart from uniforms, is rarely symbolic in any way. One of the most important functions of clothing at any time before the second half of the twentieth century was to show social status. Perhaps the last example of instantly recognizable status clothing in modern times is the fur coat, for although designer clothes might be hugely expensive they are not always recognised by the ordinary person in the street. In the Roman period, there had to be a visible division between those who used clothes as a status symbol, because they could afford large quantities of expensive cloth and because they were not required to work, and those who had to have functional and practical clothing because they had to earn their living, either as slave or free. Therefore, both the amount of cloth used in the clothes and their colours would immediately say something about the wearer to the casual observer. Further elements of costume, their use controlled by law, such as the colour of the shoes or the width of stripes, would provide additional information. A wearer was therefore identified by a number of different elements: the quality of the cloth, its age, condition and colour, as well as the way the clothes themselves were worn, such as the length of the tunic, and whether it was worn unbelted. Finally, the types of clothes might identify their wearers: the freedman's cap for ex-slaves, the toga for citizens, or the shoulder capes particularly favoured by the lower classes.

Clothes also helped to identify race or nationality. Native costume was worn, particularly by women, during the first and second century at least, even by those who had a Romanised lifestyle. Rome itself must have seen many visitors wearing their traditional clothing, and in some circumstances mainstream fashion adopted or adapted items of clothing from the provinces. The clothes themselves could be imported over long distances, or were made more locally in the style of the foreign clothing. Diocletian's Edict therefore mentions clothes from Britain, Gaul, and Africa as well as Egypt and Asia Minor.

The Roman Empire is frequently considered to be a 'western' civilisation because it had provinces in what is now western Europe, but it had equal interests in eastern Europe and in fact more often looked to the east for inspiration (sometimes to the disgust of the conservatives), and eventually even its capital moved east to Constantinople. This interest in the east can also be seen in costume. At first Rome looked to Greek culture, and such items as the mantle worn by men and the gap-sleeved tunic worn by women were adopted from Greek costume, while later Rome looked to the Persians and adopted the use of highly patterned and decorated cloth. From beyond the Empire they imported gems from India and silk from China.

The most important trend in the development of Roman costume over the centuries was the gradual tendency for the body – both male and female – to be covered up. Men went from wearing short sleeved, knee-length tunics with bare legs to long-sleeved, calf-length tunics with skin-tight hose. Women, already well covered in the first century when wrapped in a mantle, ended up with only face and hands visible even in the privacy of their own home. In the east the use of patterned materials and more tailored clothes continued to evolve as the Byzantine Empire developed, and thus became part of the clothing of the medieval world.

Glossary

abolla	form of mantle
balteus	literally 'belt'; also used to describe the diagonal folds of cloth from shoulder to armpit on the toga
bardocullus	shoulder cape
bracae	a word that seems to have been used for both knee-length breeches and ankle-length trousers
byrrus	form of cape
calceus	shoe; particularly the form of shoeboot worn with the toga
caligae	openwork shoes worn by soldiers
cenatoria	a 'set' of tunic and mantle worn during late afternoon meals
chlamys	Greek form of cloak adopted by the military
consul	highest rank of Roman magistrate. Chosen annually, there were only ever two at any particular time
cucullus	shoulder cape
dalmaticus	late form of long-sleeved tunic
endromis	thick mantle worn by athletes
equestrian	a social rank (also translated as 'knight') based on a monetary qualification
fascea/fascia	literally 'bandages', used of puttees worn by men and women, and of the breastband worn by women

flabellum	fan
flammeum	flame-coloured mantle worn by brides
institia	strap or bandage, including the shoulder straps of a *stola*
knight	a social rank (also translated as 'equestrian') based on a monetary consideration
lacerna	form of cloak worn by civilians
laena	form of cloak worn by civilians
mafortium	shawl or hood worn by women
mantle	rectangle of cloth used as an outer covering
matron	respectable married woman of some social status
mitra	turban
paenula	form of cape
paludamentum	form of scarlet cloak worn by Generals
pallium/palla	mantle
pero	ankle boot
ricinium	head veil
senator	a social rank based on a monetary consideration
sagum	thick cloak that originated in the western provinces, particularly worn by soldiers and country folk
sinus	literally a fold; also used to describe the deep loop of folds on the toga across the front of the body on the right-hand side
snood	cloth or net cap worn by women to keep hair in place
soccus	cloth sock; possibly also refers to cloth shoe
soleas	shoes worn inside the house

sprang-work	a form of fabric made by knotting rather than weaving (cf crochet and knitting)
stola	female overtunic that became symbolic of a Roman matron
suffibulum	short mantle worn over the head by Vestal Virgins
synthesis	literally 'set'; taken to mean a set of tunic and mantle worn during evening meals
tablion	inset of coloured cloth on cloaks worn by court officials in the late Empire
toga	an elaborate form of mantle that became the national dress of the Roman citizen
tube-dress	form of tunic made from a tube of cloth, fastened by brooches on the shoulders
tunicus/tunica	the main garment of both man and woman, with or without sleeves
umbellam	parasol
umbo	literally 'boss'; used to describe the small loop of cloth produced just above the waist on some of the early forms of draping the toga
vittae	ribbons worn round the head for religious reasons
umbracula	parasol

References

In most cases, the translations have been taken from the Loeb editions, with some modifications, particularly in the matter of the terminology used for clothing. The translation of Soranus is taken from that of O. Temkin, and of Vegetius from the tranlsation by N. P. Milner. The translation of Tertullian is that published in the *Ante-Nicene Christian Library (vol 28)* and that of Sulpicius Severus from the *The Nicene and post-Nicene Fathers (2nd series, vol 2)*.

d. = died; fl. = flourished

name	abbreviation	title	date
Ammianus Marcellinus	History		d.400
Apuleius	Ass	The golden ass	fl.160
Aulus Gellius		Attic nights	d.175
Cato	Farming	On farming	d.149 BC
Catullus		Poems	d.54 BC
Cicero	Letter	Letters to friends	d.43 BC
	Catiline	Second speech against Catiline	
	Soothsayers	Response to the soothsayers	
	Clodius	Against Clodius and Curio	
Claudian	Honorius	On the fourth consulship of Honorius	fl.400
	Eutropius	Against Eutropius	
		Epithalamium	
	Rufinus	Second book against Rufinus	
	Probinus	On the consulship of Probinus	
	Stilicho	On Stilicho's consulship	
Columella	Farming	On farming	fl.50
Digest		Extracts of Roman law	
Festus			fl.150
Fronto		Letters	d.168
Horace	Sat.	Satires	d.8 BC
		Letters	
		Epodes	
Josephus		Jewish wars	
Juvenal	Sat	Satires	d.130

Martial	Ep.	Epigrams	d.102
OP		Oxyrhynchus papyri	
Ovid		Art of Love	d.17
		Ibis	
	Meta	Metamorphoses	
	Remedies	Remedies of love	
Persius	Sat	Satires	d.62
Petronius	Saty	Satyricon	fl.60
Pliny	Nat. Hist.	Natural histories	d.79
Pliny the Younger		Letters	d.113
Plautus		Epidicus	d.184 BC
		Comedy of asses	
Propertius		Elegies	d.16 BC
Prudentius		Daily round	fl.400
		Mansoul	
Quintilian	Instit.	The education of the orator	d.95
Seneca		Debates	d.65
Servius		Commentary on the Aeneid	fl.390
SHA		Scriptores Historiae Augustae; a collection of biographies by various authors	late third – early fourth century
Sidonius		Letters	d.488
Soranus		Gynecology	early second century
Statius		Silvae	d.96
Strabo		Geography	early first century
Suetonius		Lives of the Caesars	d.160
Sulpicius Severus		Dialogues	d.425
Tertullian	Mantle	On the mantle	d.220
	Crown	On the military crown	
Tibullus		Elegies	d.18 BC
Varro		On farming	d.27 BC
Vegetius		On military science	fl.386

Weaving terminology

A loom, of whatever design, is basically a wooden frame to support and to keep taut the threads used during weaving. The threads that hang vertically are called the **warp**. The thread that is passed backwards and forwards horizontally is called the **weft**. Cloth is woven by passing the weft over one thread and under the next, so that on a loom there must be some threads towards the front and some towards the back. The gap between these two sets of threads is called the **shed**. The threads at the back are attached by loops to a rod at the front so that by pulling this rod forward, the back threads can be pulled in front of the other threads. The rod that changes which threads are to the front is called the **heddle rod**. Two or more heddle rods can be used to bring forward the threads in different orders, which will produce patterns in the cloth itself.

The warp can be prepared for the loom by the production of a **starting border**. This is a narrow braid woven using small cards instead of a loom, but on one side of the braid, the weft is left hanging in very long loops. The finished braid is attached to the bar along the top of the loom, and the loops are cut at the bottom so that the back half of the loops drops back and the front half is brought forward, thus producing the shed. The last warp threads on either side which will form the edge of the woven cloth are often bundled together to create a strong edge. This woven edge is called the **selvage** or **selvedge**.

The different groupings of warp and weft threads produce different **weaves**, such as **tabby** where the weft passes under and over single warp threads, and **half-basket** where the weft passes under and over two warp threads. Other weaves include basket weave, two-over-two twill, herringbone twill and diamond twill.

When woven, the cloth (often already in the shape of a garment) was sent to the **fuller** for finishing. The natural grease in sheep's wool (**lanolin**) was removed, if not required to make the cloth waterproof, and the cloth was shrunk. To make woollen cloth softer, the **nap** was raised; this involved running something with a rough surface over the cloth to pull up the fibres slightly without catching the threads themselves, producing a fluffy surface. The nap was then trimmed to a even height, giving a finish similar to that found on modern blankets.

Sprang

Sprang-work is a method of producing cloth by knotting rather than weaving (cf crochet and knitting). It was carried out on a small frame, with adjacent threads twisted round each other.

Select bibliography

There are few up-to-date books available that study Roman costume in any detail. One of the most recent is *The World of Roman Costume* edited by J.L. Sebesta and L. Bonfante (1994, Winconsin). This contains a number of articles written on a wide range of topics under the categories of clothing, hair and accessories, literary evidence and provincial clothing. There are very few detailed discussions of Roman costume published in English, and the books written by L.M. Wilson, although now partially outdated, are still the most comprehensive. *The Clothing of the Ancient Romans* (1938, Baltimore) describes both male and female mainstream costume while *The Roman Toga* (1924, Baltimore) concentrates, as the name suggests, on a single item. A more recent study of the toga has been written by S. Stone ('The toga: from national to ceremonial costume' in *The World of Roman Costume*).

Female costume has also been discussed in *The World of Roman Costume*, including symbolism in clothing and bridal clothing, while the *stola* has been studied by B. Scholz in *Untersuchungen zur Tracht der Römischen Matrona* (1992, Cologne). *The Jewellery of Roman Britain* by C. Johns gives a good overview of all the jewellery types found in the province (1996, London). A study by N. Fuentes on the military tunic includes a discussion on the knotted tunic ('The Roman military tunic' in *Roman Military Equipment: the Accoutrements of War,* edited by M. Dawson, 1987, Oxford).

J.P. Wild has written two articles on the clothing of the north-west provinces, both published in German journals. These are 'Clothing in the north-west provinces of the Roman Empire' in *Bonner Jahrbücher* 68 (1968) and 'The clothing of Britannia, Gallia Belgica and Germania Inferior' in *Aufstieg und Niedergang der Römischen Welt* 12.3 (1985). The clothing from Gaul is also discussed in *Costumes et Textiles en Gaule Romaine* by G. Roche-Bernard (1993, Paris). Costumes from the eastern Empire are discussed by B. Goldman and L. Roussin in *The World of Roman Costume,* while the elaborate costume of Palmyra is described in *The Art of Palmyra* by M.A.R. Colledge (1976, London).

The book *Ancient Danish Textiles from Bogs and Burials* by M. Hald (1980, Copenhagen) describes in detail the clothes found in Danish bogs, some of which are of Roman date, while there are a number of books cataloguing collections of cloth fragments from Egypt, including *Looms and Textiles of the Copts* by D.L. Carroll (1988, California Academy of Science) and *The Roman Heritage: Textiles from Egypt and the Eastern Mediterranean 300 to 600 AD* by J. Trilling (1982, Washington). Further detailed articles on textiles (of all periods) can be found in the series of published papers of the Symposium on Archaeological Textiles in North Europe (NESAT).

Index

Note: page references in bold indicate figures; there may also be relevant text on these pages